"Christopher Rosales' wri  nt and dirty with street-leve):
think Kendrick Lamar's _____ and Domino's "Getto Jam." These are stories from the stoops, laundromats, canals and alleyways, that show how a community weaves narrative webs to understand their own truths. So, *here we go, here we go as the tune starts to bloom.*"

—Steven Dunn, author of
Potted Meat and *water & power*

"If all stories are really either about someone leaving town or someone getting to town, then *Word is Bone* is, pretty much, all stories, but in a way that's so particular to southern California and the nineties that you'll find yourself looking down at your own feet, expecting them to be wrapped in June's cowboy boots."

—Stephen Graham Jones, author of
Mapping the Interior and *Mongrels*

A Broken River Books Original
Broken River Books
12205 Elkhorn Ct.
El Paso, TX 79936

ISBN: 978-1-940885-50-6
Printed in the USA.

WORD
IS
BONE

by
Christopher David Rosales

BROKEN RIVER BOOKS
EL PASO, TX

In the seminal crime novel The Last Good Kiss, *James Crumley writes: "You can't go home again even if you stay there . . ." but when it comes to some homes, we feel we've never left even after we've gone. This book is dedicated to Clearwater, but we all know that means Paramount, CA, Los Angeles County. And it's dedicated to my family, the family that's been there for over 100 years. The family that will call that city home for many more years to come.*

"Some say he's doing the obituary mambo,

some say he's hanging on the wall,

perhaps this yarn is the only thing that holds this man

together,

some say that he was never here at all."

—Tom Waits, "Swordfishtrombone"

ONE

Brenton said:

I don't think Junie came back just to bury his pops, to win that little girl or even to kill that man. I think he came back for this—to get people talking about him again. Hell, man. I think he'd been losing momentum.

It was 1999. He'd been my best friend since we was kids but I hadn't seen him in as long as the rest of them—ten years, maybe. June, a musician, thought life wasn't worth living if it weren't worth singing a song or telling a story about. He wasn't dramatic in the way he moved his hands, or in the way he moved his face, neither, he was dramatic in his choices of where to be and when to be there, and who to be there with.

So I wouldn't call it a shock to see him walking out of Starlight liquor with a bottle of whiskey in his hand,

1

all casual. More like a phenomenon you know to watch out for. Like an eclipse. If anything, it was a shock that he hadn't already taken the big step and claimed Kiddy. What really shocked me wasn't that it was still summer and Junie was particular about only drinking light liquors until Labor Day even though he was carrying whiskey, but that he looked like he had on a costume.

Now to get what I'm saying you have to've seen him before he took off, dressed just like me. People sometimes said we was brothers of another mother—I'm a lot darker than he is—because we even traded clothes. So like that day, for one, I was driving the roach coach but I never put on my uniform till I'm working, so I had on some fat-laced Nike Cortes, some Ben Davis jeans, and the jacket to match. I had my C hat. It's got a C on it for Cincinnati but everyone knows I represent Clearwater.

I couldn't pull over cause I was on my way to pick up a body and besides like I said it was hard to believe that was Junie. He had on tight jeans and cowboy boots. Had on a white t-shirt and a red and black lumberjack. And mostly, what was different was the set of his jaw. He looked hard, man. Like homies look right after they been let out the pen. Like the next man they meet could be the one to do them in. He still had the red facial hair—girls round town

2

used to call him June Bug—but now he looked intense. Dude looked like his face was on fire. He had a mustache like one of those cowboy ones with a fat soul-patch beneath his bottom lip.

He must have saw me staring—I nearly rear-ended the Cutlass stopped to turn left—but Junie stared right through me like I wasn't there as he crossed in front of traffic and went on down to the building, the one where we all used to live together. The one where I still live.

Like I said, I was on my way to pick up a body. I'm somewhat of an entrepreneur, see, and my latest business has been the most successful by far. Before this, I had a roach coach I operated out front of Progress Park, selling Twizzlers to the teenagers at the ballgames in the evenings, selling burritos to construction workers busy bitching by dawn. Then the city shut me down because I was taking sales from the snack-shack. I'd seen the bitch chewing her stale stock of big-league, leaning against her lukewarm vat of corndog batter, giving me the eye. She'd begun rolling her cage down in the eighth, then the seventh, finally the sixth, before I got canned. Anyway, how I got into this business is I got an old high school buddy that's a cop and he knows I have this old tank, this van I used to use as the roach coach, and he tells me about the city contracting transporters.

On this particular day he tells me about the gig, he's chilling at the park to police the yearly football game between the boys in Dogpatch and the Eastsiders, cause you know them gangbangers sometimes enjoy the violence of football more than the sport. There's a bunch of bald heads running around on the grass and all their girls and buddies are gathered around the field shouting. There's more than one big gray boombox on more than one side of the field, blasting more than one rap song or oldie but goodie.

My friend's got his shiny cop sunglasses on and he tilts them down his nose.

"Transporters?" I ask. "What do I gotta transport?"

He's all, "Dead dudes." And he puts his glasses back with a finger and crosses his arms smiling. "What do you think? Cool, right?"

His radio is chirping off and I don't have time to tell him what I think about it. Which is that it gives me the creeps.

He had to roll out right then so, technically, I didn't say no thanks. It didn't take long for the bills to hit the mailbox. A few weeks later, and there I was, on my way to pick up another dead body, and driving right past my old best friend.

* * *

I stopped down the block from the city morgue, put my uniform on in the coach, and ran the shaver over my face in the rearview mirror. Then I parked where I was supposed to, around back by the utility door, and headed on inside.

"Hey, Mary," I told Mary, the girl who works the desk. She said hold on to someone on the phone and set it down. She smiled and came around the desk to take my paperwork.

"Your new uniform looks good." She's pretty cute when she's sitting down, but boy beneath the waist it's like a different girl. Like god mixed up—gave a ballerina the ass of a bailiff. "My friend on the phone says she's hoping you'll call me again."

"People hope that about my clients, too. Wouldn't it ruin the surprise to know?" I checked the slot for the clipboard that wasn't there. "Let me guess, you aren't ready yet?"

"Wouldn't want to keep him waiting," she said, meaning, *why the hell do you keep me waiting when you're the type to worry so much about a dead dude?* But she laughed and took the phone up again and went back to talking on it, which is her favorite hobby.

"Ahem," I said, all butler-like.

"Oh, right." She got back up and came back around the desk, which took her a while. She handed me the clipboard. "Mr. Walker."

Mr. Walker? I thought. As in Junie? But I'd seen him just that day. I shook the dark thoughts loose of my head.

Before I was through the door she was back on the phone. She didn't seem even to talk that much in person, but the one time I talked to her on the phone I eventually had to pretend my battery died to get some sleep.

It didn't occur to me until I was headed down the dark hallway to the cooler that Mr. Walker could be Junie's pops. The morgue had a wall of what looks like refrigerator doors, only they're square and got locks on them. I walked down the line scanning for 11A. Turned the combination.

The cold hits you in the face and makes your eyes all tight, every time. I don't know why but I always think of death as being warm and so I don't really like that part of the job. When your eyes reheat and throb the beat of your heart, you can see the zipper running straight down the bag into the dark, and the shape of the body in there.

I raised my hand to the cold zipper and started to tug. It was down about halfway past the bridge of the nose, when I thought Junie might not have liked me doing that. He

6

was always territorial. I wheeled the dude out and said see ya to Mary who took the phone from her ear long enough to say, "I screen my phone calls, you know. If you call make sure and dial star eighty-two so I know to answer."

I loaded Junie's pops into the back of the roach coach and said, *I'll be with you in a second, Sir,* and shut the double doors on him.

I like to take the uniform off whenever I can, so I stepped out of it. It's like a jump suit or a mechanic's outfit. I wasn't told what to wear so I took it on myself—professionality is key as an entrepreneur—to have a logo made up and a uniform put together. The roach coach had huge windows in the sides to pass food through, so I had those painted black and had the logo painted there.

Charon's Ferry Transportation Services.

I had got it embroidered on the chest of the jumpsuit, too. I had found the "Charon's Ferry" part in the encyclopedia at the library. The "Transportation Services" part I came up with myself.

So I was taking the dude to the mortuary but as usual I couldn't stand the drive. You can only watch the same streets for so long: the old houses in the Sans, the chicken shacks hidden beneath blue tarps in the barrio, the cluckers at the payphones by the giant donut-topped shop in Compton. And the drive was quiet with the windows up, but awkward quiet cause I still felt like someone's with me.

So I said, "How's Mrs. Walker been? Oh. Right. I guess her name's not Mrs. Walker no more, but maybe you all kept in touch?"

Tuning the radio to the oldies station, I said, "You like oldies, right? Me too. What am I thinking? June probably got his taste from you. Art Laboe's show is still the bomb. That DJ must be what, like, a hundred? I ever tell you my mamma named me Brenton after Brenton Woods? Yup. She said my pops would always sing that song Oogum Boogum to her. You know that one? *Highheel boots hiphugger suits?* Man, the way you all used to dress was a trip."

It didn't take long to get to the mortuary, and when I did I pulled around back in the alley. It always smells like the pier back there cause there's this Mariscos restaurant on the other side of the alley and their dumpster's always full and open and buzzing with flies. I made the mistake of looking in there one time. There was a pile of shrimp up to the top, maggots all squirming in it, like they thought the shrimps was their parents.

I wheeled Junie's pops to the back door and pushed the buzzer. Nothing happened and after a long time I pushed the buzzer again. Finally the door opened.

"What's going on?" I asked Sam.

"I wish I could say it's dead in here." Sam's an interesting guy. He takes on a real dry attitude, which makes sense, his line of work. But he's huge, real huge, like has to stoop under doorways and walk sideways through them too, and instead of just seeming respectful, and serious and all, he comes off a little like Frankenstein. "But we've got a situation. The family of the deceased was told the deceased would be here by two." He kind of sighed everything he said and, after, nodded slowly with his lips tight the way you do to console someone. But he especially sighed when using his politically correct terms around my ears. *Family of the deceased* sounded to me like a bunch of zombies, and I always told him so. Not this time though. He was bugging out. The family of the deceased had been haunting his workplace for over an hour. "I called the morgue many, many times, Brenton. And the line was busy."

"You know Mary, man, she's always chatting it up. Help me get him inside."

We hadn't gotten far down the hall when I realized I wasn't wearing my uniform. "Fuck."

"Pardon?" Sam pursed his lips to keep from sighing.

I looked down at my jeans and t-shirt in the yellow glow of those fancy lamps on the walls. "My—"

That's when the "family of the deceased" surrounded us. It was two women and a man and all of them were about the same place on the middle-age ladder that looks the same from forty-five to sixty. "This is unbelievable," the man kept saying, and each time one of the women would try to talk he'd say, "Let me handle this, Norma," or, "Let me handle this, Kate," and then just say again, "Unbelievable." I could hear their kids playing somewhere in the lobby, laughing, which sounded real creepy in that cold, and dark, quiet, building. I took my proper position behind Sam, who was saying, "This area is for workers only, folks," with that same sad nod at the end. "I'm very, very sorry."

The one called Norma finally spat out before the man could shut her up that they'd flown out here from Arizona because their nephew had hijacked their brother-in-law's body.

"I'll be damned," Kate said, a hand on a belly the size of a basketball and stuffed into high-waisted jean-shorts, "if his ex-wife is gonna get to run this cat and pony show."

"Horse," the man told her. "I don't believe it."

The one named Norma thumbed the strap of her halter-top back up her freckled shoulder. "Now you two know

10

Maggie had nothing to do with this. It's that crazy son of theirs, July."

"June," the man said.

Junie. I didn't want to believe what I was hearing. I'd never met Junie's pops before. He'd left Junie and his moms way back when we was still kids. But Junie liked to talk about him like he still saw him all the time. He always told stories about his pops. Good stories. Only thing was, the stories didn't always add up. And here he was on the gurney. I wondered if, knowing Junie, he was going to force his pops to add up.

"Can you believe that son of a bitch?" The man passed his eyes up and down my clothes, and I was already shaking my head, wishing more than anything that I hadn't forgotten that uniform folded on the passenger seat of the Ferry. The man was wearing a lime green polo shirt and was in a constant fight to keep it tucked, and his pleated khaki shorts showed too much pasty leg for any man, wearing or seeing. He punched one hand into a pocket and pointed a finger of the other at me. "And another thing. What kind of place hires a," he looked at Sam, still wagging a finger at me, or meaning to but veering off toward a lamp on the wall, "a goddang gangbanger. Carting our beloved dead, deceased I mean, dearly departed? A gangster! Unbelievable."

11

"I'm sorry, Sir," I said. "But, I ain't no gangbanger." And I never had been. But I was too embarrassed to be pissed. My face was hot, my gut empty, my hands shaky, so I stuffed them in my baggy pockets and made fists. I tried to explain that I had a uniform somewhere but he just kept shaking his head and finally stomped down the hall, punched one of those fancy yellow lamps on the wall as he went.

"Honey," Norma yelled, and chased after him.

"You guys!" Then Kate ran off too, still palming that belly like it might fall off.

You could hear them yelling at the kids to come on. Sam and I stood there, awkward and quiet, staring at that crooked lamp on the wall, keeping Junie's dead pops company. All I wanted to do was apologize to him, about forgetting my uniform. But I couldn't talk to him in front of Sam. I sort of thought out the apology in my head. I promised I'd do a better job next time, not that it'd make a difference to him or his. I promised respect. I asked him was it okay if it never got back to his son Junie about me not wearing my uniform. And then I stopped because I realized I was thinking that he could hear my thoughts, assuming ghosts knew our promises and if we broke them. That whole idea was too heavy and then I wished even more that

12

I could just go back to talking to him out loud, like all the other dead ones. In the end though, I was too embarrassed, and I was extra ashamed of not saying nothing. We just stood there, Sam and me, and Junie's pops on the gurney.

Eventually Sam broke the silence with a sigh. "I'd better take him down to the workshop now."

Sam came around to my side of the gurney and I had to stand back against the wall to make him some room, but when he wheeled that man away the hall felt empty, long, and dark.

Well. So. That's what went down. That's how I knew it was true—June was back.

TWO

When the cops let June leave the sub-station, after the incident with Kiddy, he took the most direct route home, down Clearwater Avenue, past the church, the grammar school, and then Kiddy's Junior High.

He had just finished lighting a cigarette and tossed the match aside when a Samoan man driving a golf-cart rolled up on him. The man was wearing all black and he was so wide that he took up both seats. There was a gold shield screenprinted onto his chest, and a bleach-splatter across the belly.

The guard kept his head leaned back like he was constantly being tugged out of a nap and he regarded June from behind polarized glasses. "I went to high-school with you, fool."

"You did?" June asked, and scratched his bald head, regretting the question instantly.

"You're going to have to get out of here." His lips were chapped and when he breathed he showed the fleshy inside of the bottom one.

June was still walking. The man shifted the cart into gear, turned, and rode up alongside June with the electric motor humming. June lengthened his stride and the cart whined just to keep up.

"Sir," the guard said. "You're going to have to stay off these premises."

While he walked June looked through the chainlink fence at the empty soccer field, at the open doors to the gymnasium. He could hear basketballs bouncing in there, a rim rattle. He took a drag off his cigarette. "I'm gone."

The guard lurched the cart to a stop. "No adults allowed to loiter round the premises."

June took a last drag off the cigarette, tossed it into traffic flying by, called without looking back, "I'm off the fucking premises."

He thought he heard what the guard whispered into the CB-radio, though he was much too far to be able. In the Rosewood diner, halfway home, he stopped for dark coffee in a just as dark booth, and he heard the waitresses loitering behind the register, gossip hissing like a pit of snakes. He stopped in the carnicería near home and when he approached the counter with a bag of chicharones and a bottle of hot sauce in one hand, two limes balanced in the palm of the other, the woman stopped speaking mid-sentence. She was a light woman with a slight mustache. She had been speaking Spanish. He didn't speak much Spanish but he was sure he had understood her by some feat of heightened senses. This must be what a dog feels like, he thought, right before an earthquake.

Voices blew hot over him like the Santa Ana winds. His eyes dried up. He learned to breathe through his teeth whenever he heard voices coming. *June molested that little girl, don't care what she say, and prob'ly killed that woman of all women, Rosalina. Spanky gonna hurt him for that.*

As a musician, he'd hoped they'd all talk about him. Thrived on it, even. He would have been bored, otherwise. But now it was as if there were so many different people singing his favorite song that they formed one frayed and hairy braid of dissonant music that he could not untie from or tie up to any other, so that those songs, all songs, felt lost from him if he did not eliminate the noise, the feedback, the microphone and the speaker—himself.

And the gossip finally sent him packing. No one knew to where. No one cared. It was far more interesting to speculate until finally even speculation became a bore. Then they forgot all about him. And his dried up eyes. And his teeth bared just to breathe.

Now it had been ten years, when June finally saw Kiddy again. She was cutting another young woman's hair—both sitting on the old diving board, straddling it with feet dangling over the dry poolbed—and Kiddy had scissors poised in one hand. The other girl wagged a rolled up screenplay through the air, insisting that Kiddy call her Daisy. She was also insisting that Kiddy use the ruler she currently wielded like a butcher's knife, insisting that industry standard was a matter of eighth inches, not quarters, and the board was creaking under what little the two of them could have weighed. Whatever that weight was, June would have said most of it was that new girl's. Kiddy looked as tiny as the night he'd left her. When she'd been only fifteen. And when he'd first admitted to himself that he loved her.

It had been a hot Friday in the summer of 1989. June was toting his guitarcase solemnly through the breezeway. He'd trimmed away most of his goatee, styled it and the mustache in what seemed an effort to appear artistic but on his strong jaw and with his hard features—you were constantly aware of skull, of bone—he looked more cold and calculating than any true artist ought to. Perhaps even piratic.

Kiddy was sitting in the evening light in her open window with foam headphones on her ears, hunched over one upraised knee and painting her big toenail blue.

June didn't stop, didn't seem to notice her, but that was because he didn't seem to notice anything when worrying through a coming performance. He watched the cement, eyes tracking side to side in that haunting but handsomely formed skull, as if he were reading the reviews to his show there—a show still to come in a dark bar around the corner and performed for a few local drunks, none of whom could string together enough words for a review even if allowed to lean toward the profane.

Kiddy tugged a wire and an earphone popped off her ear. "Hey."

June looked around as if he'd imagined this voice, a groupie manifested out of thin air, before he spotted her in the window and smiled.

"I'm listening to your tape." She jiggled her Walkman at him.

"I'm on my way to that gig."

"No one says 'gig.'" She hopped out the window and walked her mother's walk toward him, her bare feet padding the cement. "Do they?" She'd obviously meant to ask this last bit to his face, but she did not quite know her mother's method for a graceful terminus, and left a blue scrape on the cement when she stubbed her toe.

She'd adopted as an afterthought an improvised hipslung stance, and June was regrettably reminded of choosing some player last at recess. He said, "Isn't it past your bedtime?"

"Take me," she said.

"I don't know—"

He hadn't known why he'd taken her, either. He had known it couldn't end well. Now, June said, "Kiddy," as if he were trying to remind her who she'd been then, trying to call a friend back from a concussion, saying not *do you recognize me,* but *do you recognize where you are, and who?* She had just begun to swing her feet but now froze.

"Nobody calls me Kiddy anymore." She didn't look up. *Snip snip.*

"I ain't nobody."

"You ain't somebody, neither."

The other young woman said, "But everybody calls you Kiddy." Kiddy took the ruler and dug it deep into the other's scalp to check the length of a strand.

19

"Ow." Daisy swatted Kiddy's hand with the rolled up screenplay.

June held a cassette tape out over the empty space between them. "I brought you an old tape of mine."

"I don't listen to music."

"You don't what?"

"Tell him I don't listen to music anymore."

The other girl said, "She doesn't listen to music anymore." She pouted her glossy lips at him and said, "Hi. I'm Daisy Columbine."

Kiddy said, "She's Linda Contreras."

June ignored them. "What do you mean you don't listen to music?"

"Tape player got stolen. Doesn't matter. I've gone into movies. We've got an audition end of next week."

Daisy raised her chin high and turned away as if to present her good side for a picture but June could tell she just wanted to show him the mole on her left cheek. It was a little smeared but aside from that it looked good on her. "I'm a screenwriter," she said. "But we've both been told we could be actresses."

"Famous actresses," Kiddy shot at him, as if there could be one without the other and she wanted no mistakes made which she'd take first.

20

"By who?" June asked.

The question stalled them. They looked at each other for an answer, and their squints made it obvious to June that they'd mutually invented a truth and forgotten it was invention. June took the opportunity of their puzzlement to look around the courtyard, the empty pool, up at the sky above them. He had the right place. The right girl. But this wasn't the reception he'd expected. He'd figured at worst she'd have a lingering high school sweetheart he'd have to chase off to prove he wasn't playing.

When he looked back at Kiddy she had a wing of Daisy's hair in one hand and was parting strands from it with the pinky of the other, the scissors spread wide. She seemed to be concentrating harder than she had to, like this was all some ruse put on to frustrate him, to get him back for leaving without saying goodbye. Maybe the other one, Daisy, was in on it too. Maybe she was giggling somewhere inside some of that extra flesh. He thought the sorry act would crumble the longer he stood there.

"What happened to music?" he asked. Because music had mattered so much to both of them, to all he could call "them." Who they'd been. What they'd had. Whatever that was.

June's set at the Barrel house had taken about an hour and Kiddy was the only one in the place that saw every second of it. He returned her favor by watching her back. It seemed some awkward serenade, constantly under threat of being broken up by her bashfulness, by his shame, by the bar's regulars mumbling their discontent that the jukebox was shutoff. June had a beautiful voice, anyone would have said so, but he played music softer and sadder than any in that place wanted to hear on a Friday night. When Kiddy leaned forward to hear him over the noise he could see the waistband of her panties show—something silver caught the light, shimmered like a blade of glass, disappeared like one too.

He took a drink of the gin sitting on the stool beside his own—it was summer so no dark, no whiskey—drained the glass, set it on the floor, and called her up. He leaned over and whispered in her ear while she tried to hide her face behind her hands upraised to hold the microphone. "Which one of my songs you know best?"

She said, "All of them," and her voice came over the PA. The microphone whistled until she pulled her hands away and stuffed them in her back pockets. She looked at him and mouthed the words, *I know all of them best.*

She took a seat with her feet tucked back around the stool as if to hide their nakedness.

He began a percussive arpeggio, strutted it back and forth like the song had a decision to make, and he was offering only one of two chords. As if one thing were being weighed against something else he did not know yet. He had his hand clamped high on the neck of the guitar, frozen and black for the light in his eyes. He could just make out the exaggerated gestures of the drunken audience struggling to place the song. An ear cupped, a raised drawn-on brow.

When she began to sing, she came in right on time. He closed his eyes tight, seemed to gather courage to face the source of that hot velvet being dragged up his back, that confusion of senses that had him drinking music like syrup and hearing it like a breath on his neck.

She sang mostly with her eyes closed and that was what did him in. Not because of the neck she arched to him or the collarbone she lightly thrummed with her fingertips, or her expression as if amidst all the drunks growing drunker she'd found some measure of peace, but because with her eyes closed he could stare at her and, the whole song through, he did.

When she got to the second verse she brushed a strand of hair behind an ear. He followed its fall down her shoulder, to the pink indentation from the bra beneath her arm, to the milkwhite flesh there when she raised an arm to grip her hair, and he could smell her and he was drunk on that smell, drunker than a bottle could make him. Drunk to his bones. Slurring his body language.

She leaned her weight on her arms, elbows locked, and gripped the seat's edge between her thighs. The muscle at the back of her arm made a small horseshoe. He could see a piece of her panties rise above the waist of her jeans and saw what had shimmered there earlier, a large safety-pin. He shut his eyes on it and told himself he wouldn't look at her anymore.

He remembered reading somewhere that the man who creates the music is imposing order, and he remembered agreeing, but, now, he felt instead that order was being imposed on him. If the soundhole of the guitar ran straight into the depths of the man behind it, then this little girl's hand was small enough to reach inside. But he'd make sure she'd find no music. She'd find wailing where there ought to be singing, bashing where rhythm was required, long rough fingernails plucking rusted strings, and he would defy her to make it into something pretty.

The last bridge was being built out of the song from scratch. It was taking them further out into the air, away from this city, and with no city yet to build themselves toward. She was searching for the place the bridge would end, and the song, or the man playing it, seemed to say *here, here,* but she shook her head that it wasn't the right place. Through this door. Down this dark passage. Who will be waiting? What?

They didn't reach the final chorus, more like they fell into it. They'd left the bridge behind them with the help of a new key, opened a door onto a new city to move through, where they both, man and girl, could move hand in hand, unashamed. She began to rock forward and back, perched on the stool and at times near to falling. He could see her smooth feet, the toes stretched against a crossbar, the fade in the skin at the sole from pink to white.

When the song ended he stood and put the guitar in its case, the jukebox blared something bassy, and she was asking, pleading really, "How'd I do?"

He wouldn't look at her, as if he was already sure of, and had decided against, what he would see. "You did fine, okay? Let's get out of here." He'd shut his guitarcase with a loud *skitch.*

Kiddy snipped some hair away from Daisy's bangs. Whenever one of the girls moved at all, the diving board made a creaking sound that made June's teeth ache. "I'm not leaving til you tell me why you stopped singing."

"Well then you can go," Kiddy said. "Because I already told you. They stole my tape player."

"Movies? Just like that? But you loved music."

"They stole my tape player, they didn't steal my VCR. Besides. . ." She looked at him with her eyebrows high at opposite ends ". . . there's a ten-year streak I got going that you ain't been knowing what I loved or what I didn't."

He chucked his tape frisbeelike into the pool and it cracked on the cement wall. The insides unspooled like something you'd find squirming in a dog's gut. He flared his mustache with a pursed lip, took the flannel off one sleeve at a time, and laid it over one arm. He was cooler, but cool wasn't calm. He stood there in a t-shirt and jeans and cowboy boots, Daisy giggling at him. She smiled and her cheeks swelled, shining, increasing the mass of her face by half. "You look like James Dean," she said. "Or Martin Sheen in *Badlands*."

He took the old safety-pin from where he'd fastened it through the buttonhole of his flannel, batted the shining thing up and down in his palm. "I saved this."

"What is it?" Kiddy asked.

After their performance at the Barrel house, June had tried to escape to his apartment alone but Kiddy couldn't be ditched. She'd trailed him only because of his longer stride and her bare feet. She came up to his place, closed the door softly with a hand on the knob and one on the frame. And then she turned around, already unwinding her elbows, and her shirt coming up over her head.

He set his drink down on the kitchen counter and told her to get out. "Don't bring your mamma's business in here."

But he spoke too soft. He'd had too many drinks. Her eyelids blinked shut so slow he thought they'd never open and when they did he looked away. That's when she crouched down with her hands on her jeans and stood straight with them round her ankles. She stepped out of them like they were a puddle. Her finger tugged the elastic of her panties at her thigh. "What does that mean? That this," she hugged herself, then she pointed through the wall, down the stairs, into her mother's house where a man lit a cigarette on the stove and her mother was naked and blurry in the background, "You think this is like that?"

She stood on her toes as if she were creeping in the dark, afraid of what she was stepping through or into, but still she came on. She reached her arms behind her back and her small breasts pushed against her bra. When she dropped her arms the bra fell away. She backed him against

27

the kitchen counter, where bottles stood in various states of emptiness arranged from light to dark. He wouldn't look at her breasts. He was telling himself not to. "Would you get out of here already? Alright? Leave me alone."

She seemed to be holding back tears by force, recruiting the muscles of her cheeks, her jaw, her chin. He looked at the waist of her panties, the safety-pin sparkling there. She saw him staring and looked down at the safety-pin as if she'd forgotten it.

"What's that for?" he asked.

She undid it, had it clutched in her fist when she stood again on tiptoe, came on, took his bottom lip between both of hers, and pressed both fists to his chest. He smelled the coconut shampoo. Felt the sharp pain in his chest.

He pushed her away.

She'd pressed the straightened safety-pin into his chest, dug it far as it would go into his sternum. The pin stood between thumb and forefinger, vibrating like a guitar string.

She bit her bottom lip so hard that when she let it loose there were deep red hatches all across its length, but then she no longer looked like she would cry. Her eyes lacked the shine, her mouth was slack, and she held up her chin as if she were studying him. She pointed at him like she'd caught him in a lie. "I did good. I did better than fine."

"You're right." He was breathing through his teeth when he tugged the pin free. "But I can't do this."

"You're mean." She covered her breasts with a lone hugging arm, the other she used to cover her face.

He gripped the underside of the bar like a man in an earthquake, and begged his brows downward, "Kiddy?"

"Kiddy?" He begged her once again, standing alongside those two girls suspended out in the air of that empty pool. He thumbed the mysterious safety-pin stuck through the buttonhole of his flannel, and considered pricking himself til he had returned to the right place. "It's the pin. See?"

She looked at it, then back to Daisy's hair. "Oh yeah."

He snorted and looked away and stuck a thumb out to say, *man, she's taking me for a ride.* There was no one to say it to. The courtyard was cool and empty. He looked back at her and crouched down, elbows on his knees so that his face and Kiddy's were in line, with Daisy's smiling face between them. He was conscious of the empty space of the pool below, conscious of his weight drawing him forward onto his toes. "Just like that, huh?"

She said nothing. *Snip. Snip.*

Daisy quit smiling and resumed an openmouthed pout. She seemed to be wanting to say to the world, *kiss me,* but June'd be first in line to slap her instead. Both of them. Kiddy's feet hung suspended above the dirty poolbed for a moment before they resumed their swinging.

Well, there was hope. Not everything had changed. Kiddy still liked to paint her toenails blue.

THREE

Walter said:

When Junie came to me saying he wanted his old place back I felt bad for the young man, cause his place was of course taken. And taken by the oddest ball in the poolhall, that little feminine fellow Augustine.

I knew Junie'd never done anything untoward with that little girl, and I'd seen her do things to him with her eyeballs no man who can't have some should be forced to imagine. And that fat woman's death was a freakshow. If you ask me the one the cops should've scared off was that girl Kiddy's mother. Hunh. Good looks do run in the blood. But so do other things. So on the one hand I felt bad sending Junie away all heated, but on the other hand I felt good keeping him away from that little girl Kiddy now that she wasn't such a little girl anymore.

Kayla was listening to one of her taped stories when I got in. I'd spent all afternoon figuring on how I would get that hair out the poolbed without having to climb down in it, and still hadn't figured it out. All I'd done was collect about a locket worth's of hair off the diving board and dropped that into my pocket—I was about ready to leave the girls to their own mess. When the back freezes up, I can barely push a broom. Also I could think of worse things than pretty young women's hair. Hunh. Dirty old man till a dead old man.

"What are you smiling about, Walter?" the wife asked me when I come in.

"Oh, nothing."

"I don't trust that smile," she said. "You're rubbing your hands again. You take that medicine?"

"That medicine don't do anything a drink can't do."

"Who was that you were talking to out there?"

"You remember Junie Walker?"

"You mean Junio Jiminez?"

"I mean June Walker. It's how he introduced himself his whole life."

"Well we all knew his mamma was a Mexican and she introduced him the other way."

I said, "Well mammas don't dictate the world."

32

The pitch of her voice shot high. "The hell they don't."

"You got a point." I went to the stereo she keeps in the bookshelf and paused her story. She gets real mad if I make her miss a bunch but she never rewinds cause she can't stand not to get to the end fast as fast can. "You caused a lot of trouble for that young man back then," I said, soft, so she wouldn't think I was accusing her of anything. I went around the counter into the kitchen to get a beer, opened the fridge. "You want one?"

She didn't say no.

I took two bottles of Coors from inside the door and shut the fridge. I screwed off the top of one and took it over to her.

"He deserved it." She took the beer and set it on the end table. Went back to clacking those needles. The scraping of those things made me shiver.

"But he didn't," I said. "Even the police said so." I bellied up at the counter with the unopened bottle pressed against the back of my neck.

She said, "I may have been wrong in the particulars, but you just wait and see."

There's no reasoning. I said, "I feel bad for the young man. You know he just had his daddy shipped out here from Arizona? He and his mamma got to attend services alone. She came all the way up from the Baja Peninsula. You know nobody else gonna come after what they all heard about Junie before he left."

She said, "My condolences, Walter. You can give them to him," and raised her bottle up with a pinky sticking out before she took a drink.

"Wanted his old place back," I said.

"You said no."

"I said no."

She nodded once, as if I'd followed an order. She pressed play, and the stereo started talking. She went back to clacking those knitting needles at a scarf or a sock or something neither of us would ever wear. I opened my bottle and drank. The fridge never made them cold enough, though, old as it was, so I put the bottle back inside. I was stalling. I poked around in the freezer but wasn't much in there but a bag of peas and some sugarfree popsicles. She never believed in food that wasn't fresh. Unfortunate, because she believed even less in cooking. Eventually I said, "Should have said yes and gotten that fairy out of here. You know he's into god knows what. You know, you and your sisters have been picking on real men from day one. I've taken my lumps. You may've even picked on Adam, you been around long enough." I shut the freezer.

"I'm telling you, Walter, June gives me bad feelings."

I rushed around the counter to the stereo, with one hand pressed to my stiff back, and smacked all the buttons at once with the other. The tape stopped. "These stories give you bad feelings. There's no mystery to it, Kayla. It's all laid out in front of your nose. All you got to do is sniff."

She leaned over the arm of the chair and pressed play on the stereo. The voice was all deep and warbling for a second before it got going right. "You'll see," Kayla told me. Calm. Like she hadn't heard a word I'd said.

I left because that's how I do when we're fighting because I cool down and get back later and we make up. You know how. Hunh. I took my walk around the complex spearing trash in the grass and flowerbeds with that nailstick I got, a walking stick with a couple nails pointing out the end.

The neighborhood around us ain't all that bad. It used to be dairies clear up into the sixties and when Kayla and I first settled down here after my stint stationed out in San Pedro with the Merchant Marines you could still see a lot of open yellow land, the smell of the cows making the air heavy. Whites and Mexicans would sleep around different trees in the afternoon, as if the sun or the cowsmell either one had snuck up on them and knocked them flat out in the shade. Picked their pockets of their money and their heads of worries. They looked like the men in history books. They were segregated. They were tired. They were so dirty as to already be black and white pictures. Little by little they disappeared, and all that were left were the pictures.

Nowadays our side of the street was all the working class folks. Mostly Mexicans, and mostly families. A few blacks moving in from Compton more and more each year. And it wasn't the families' faults this was where the crime was. It was the young men stalking around. But the young men got to belong to some families, I guess. And so on our side of the street it was all apartment complexes or neighborhoods of duplexes and triplexes the few miles there was to the 91 freeway. I preferred to walk on the other side of the street where it was safer.

The other side of the street was a mix of ranch style homes and California bungalows as if when they developed the place they were too far inland to have all of one, but too far from the coast to have all the other. And in general the town had that two-toned look to it. Like it wasn't a city, but also not just a neighborhood. It ain't Los Angeles but it ain't Long Beach. Not dark enough to be Compton. Not white enough to be Lakewood. It's our neighborhood. It's Clearwater.

The ranch homes mostly surrounded the old Dutch reformed church that'd bought them all up for its parishioners. Their blond kids played in the gated yard where the nicest basketball courts in the neighborhood were. Sometimes little brown kids, so skinny they could squeeze through the bars in the fence and pick up the bald basketball they thought to toss over ahead of time, would shoot around until they got caught. But the neighborhood was only this nice for round about two football fields in any direction, and then all the rest was like our side of the street again. BBQ Wing Joints and carnicerías, the signs all in Spanish, the music blaring out of the old beat up cars all in Spanish or else in that rap music's half-assed excuse for English. The train always howled its lazy complaints about carting things through us to downtown L.A. It was like the train could cross time, carting the things that make a small town off to where the sun sets in the smog, looking like those candles the old Mexican women kept behind the dirty glass of their kitchen windows. The Spanish music and the rap music and the train rattling all made a racket that never quit. Not until late evenings.

That's when I took my walks, carrying that nailstick case there were any young men about. It's young men that cause most of the trouble, you know.

But not June. Not how I ever saw things.

* * *

I was bound and determined to tell Kayla that I was moving June back in, when I got back to our place and Kayla snuggled her rump up against me. "What if I was wrong about him?"

"Now you're talking," I said to her. "What if?"

"What if I caused him all this hurt?"

She sounded all stuffed up like she had been or was about to cry.

I called her sweetheart. Honey.

"What if?" It was like she was begging me for an answer.

"You look beautiful," I told her.

She said, "Well I feel awful."

I said, "Well I guess then it works in inverse proportions."

"Seriously, Walter." I had been rubbing her behind and she smacked my hand away. She can be an awful strong woman, especially when she doesn't want any tenderness. I suggested she say sorry to Junie. It would settle her mind.

"Don't you see? Don't you see it?" She sat up in the bed. "Sorry isn't gonna save me. What if, after all these years—oh I wronged him sure, spreading all those rumors—now his father's dead, and it's just him and his mamma out here and I been blessed with a long living husband..."

I sat up in bed and it hurt my back like hell but I needed to look her in the eyes, which were frantic, the eyeshadow smudged around them, and say once and for all, "Woman, what in hell are you talking about?"

"He's come to kill me. Walter, don't you see?"

I said all I seen was a crazy old woman, and laughed and laughed. "There's no such things as mysteries." Here to kill her?

She punched her pillow to fluff it like Mike Tyson fluffs a face, and then she laid back down. I felt bad after she was quiet for a while. I knew I'd hurt her feelings. I sure couldn't sleep with her feeling bad. I just lay there, thumbed the small locket of freshcut hair in my pocket. Then I left that alone and thumbed Kayla's hair near her ear while she snored. Hunh. Dirty old man till a dead one. No mystery to any of it ever.

FOUR

Brenton said:

The next time I saw Junie I had just gotten home from work and he was stalking around his old pad. I knew he'd get it back. See, a dude like Junie, he could do that. Things just happened for, and to, him. It was always like that.

So he was smoking a cigarette and leaning on the railing in front of his open door, looking down like he was scoping shit out. When he saw me, trying to keep from dropping my bottles in those brown paper bags and trying to figure him out too, he looked disappointed. Like he'd been expecting someone else. Probably that chick. Kiddy. I was his homie, you know? And he looked disappointed.

I nodded to him and he rubbed the cigarette out on the railing, nodded back, and flicked the cigarette out into the air. It fell straight down into that dirtyass emptyass pool.

40

All the trash in there could probably go up in flames if Junie hadn't put the cigarette out, but Junie'd think of that. I heard he worked firewatch when he was out in Arizona. But he'd think of it even if he hadn't watched for fires. Junie always thought of everything.

Like, the first time he got on Spanky's bad side, it was when we were both kids. All I knew at the time was that there was a story about Junie and this Eastsider named Spanky. Still lives around here. This guy wasn't bigtime or anything like that but that meant he was meaner, trying to rack up points with EastSide *Trece*. Anyway, Spanky didn't like Junie. Lot of the cholos didn't cause he looked white but dressed like everyone else round here, which was the style to dress like a gangbanger. So Junie knew he was bound to get his ass beat, and one day the time came and Spanky saw Junie at Progress Park, which was where Spanky was bound to be drinking and dealing weed. Junie just booked it.

He hauled ass back toward Starlight Liquor, which was a long run when you think about the dude behind you might have a gun. Anyway, this I did see, he stopped at the liquor store, reached in his pocket and took out everything he had in there, which was exactly fifty cents.

"What you doing, Junie?" I asked him.

"Gotta make a phonecall. What about you?"

I held up the giant pickle I'd just bought. "Buying a pickle. Want some?"

Now keep in mind, as far as I know, all this time this badass dude Spanky is barreling after Junie, with a nina weighing his pants down for sure. But Junie finishes his call reporting a crime in progress. And, get this—not on the corner we're at, but a few blocks down the way. Then he says to me, "Give me a bite."

He eats some of the pickle and says thanks—dude was always polite—then takes off running again. Few seconds later, I'm throwing the pickle wrapper in the trashcan outside Starlight and Spanky comes huffing past me, smelling like weed-sweat and gasping. Besides being a new Eastsider he was an amateur boxer, a pretty good one. He always looked at everyone like he was predicting their moves, a spear-headed and bald snake on a back and shoulders like a stack of rocks. He was trying to hold his pants up but with a gun weighing them down watch out you don't get a show. He asks some dude at the bus-stop if a kid just ran by and, despite my trying to misdirect them, the guy tells him which way Junie went and Spanky runs full out round that corner after him.

I heard when he found Junie, Junie was just standing there waiting. Standing right in the middle of those wide ass streets near the nice houses and the Dutch Church. Spanky never quit running, just ran his fist straight into Junie's face and Junie went down. Spanky started stomping his head in, man, but right then the cops got there, broke it up, and took Spanky off to juvie.

Junie had planned to be seen, had planned to be followed, had planned to make a phonecall down to the last cent, and had planned to get punched by an all-county amateur welterweight. But that's how Junie'd always been. No doubt he'd changed since I knew him. But not in that way. Never in that way.

So when I looked back up at the breezeway, Junie's door was closed and he was gone. Just like that. And I went inside to have a bottle and go to bed cause I had to chaperone some body early the next morning. But I couldn't get my mind off the fact that Spanky was still an amateur in some ways, but now a professional in others, and he was definitely a heavyweight. Which made me think of the second time June got on Spanky's bad side.

Which was also that last night Junie saw Kiddy.

FIVE

Kiddy's mother Janine had been the prostitute of the neighborhood by both trade and reputation, and Kiddy was in some ways much like her: that is, almost pretty, fierce in demeanor but by nature weak-willed. The mother often found herself on her knees before a man, him pulling his pants up off her carpet, flaccid in sex and in countenance, spent but still with nerve to bargain. Often she worked twice as much as she had to, and often for no more than some groceries, a hairdo, a leaky faucet fixed.

After a hard day she'd hit a bottle of Boone's Farm.

"You ain't gonna be smart, sweety," she'd tell fifteen-year-old Kiddy, "and you ain't gonna be famous. Success ain't in this family's genes. I love you, is why I'm saying this. Wish someone'd loved me that much."

Saying those things seemed to make her feel better, and she took to saying them in a fatherly voice, the way one might tell a child a cliché—talent is a species of vigor—just before she'd kill her bottle and go to bed.

What everyone knew was that she was nice, but that she was bleak about the fate of her life, and her daughter's, and that people like that helped nobody. Not customers, not friends, surely not daughters—they resented themselves and inspired resentment, like someone who'd buy a losing lotto ticket before they'd lend someone else a dollar. People feared for Kiddy that, like most problems, this was her inheritance.

Janine, for her part, slept well. She'd never foreseen a threat to her business—a fair exchange to her mind, this exchange of flesh in some form, for money in some form; the sort of thing done every day by people too cowardly to admit it—but a threat to her business did come.

It came on the size of a bull and just about as demure, dressed head to toe in falsefurs and catprints, none matching, and its name was Rosalina.

Rosalina had moved into the apartment directly above, the whole stairwell echoing her steps. Within weeks Janine's customers could be heard in the breezeway, tiptoeing past Janine's door to the stairwell, strangely conscious—for once it seemed—of Janine's feelings. Janine still had her regulars of course. The beeper would vibrate on the night-stand, its LED window would glow green, and she would stare up through their thin wispy hair at the creaking ceiling furred by mold since Rosalina's arrival, listening to the sloshing of Rosalina's waterbed, thinking of some way to get even.

Kiddy spent her time at school, told girls her mother was a hairdresser. But during the summer she stayed locked in her bedroom sitting on the windowsill like some forlorn feline, her eyes closed to the sun, or focused on a TV somewhere out of sight on which she watched the old movies June lent to her, the headphones still blasting music into her ears because she'd memorized every last line.

Her mother had never involved her in business but, naturally disgusted and distrustful of men, never let the girl leave the two-bedroom apartment.

Not until that day. She'd said, "There's a first time for everything."

Kiddy turned to the man sitting on the couch, and covered her mouth at the vomit rising in her throat.

"No, sweetie," Janine said, and turned Kiddy's palm up. She pressed a large safety-pin flat, and folded the girl's

46

flushed fingers over it. "Mommy can't afford no waterbed, not that mommy would use one anyway. What's this, the eighties? No, no, no. This is the nineties, baby. We got memory foam. So just a few little pricks. We don't want a flood to carry her off. Just the landlord to kick her ass out."

Theirs was a corner apartment and at each corner was a stairwell, so Kiddy bypassed the awkward introduction to one of her mother's few remaining customers—"the dregs," Janine called them—and used the window as her passage to the stair.

You could hear June strumming as Kiddy passed Rosalina's door, elaborately nonchalant in the manner of a criminal. The posture did not seem entirely unnatural in her, albeit unfamiliar. The door was open, as always, and as always the inside musky and dark.

Most of the men came for Rosalina at night and it didn't look as if any were in there now. Not this hot afternoon at the summer's end. Didn't sound like it either. Too quiet. She seemed surprised at her headphones where they hung about her shoulders, blaring tinnily, and she shut the player off, wrapped the wires round it, and slid everything into the back pocket of her jeans, saggy not in the style of the local boys, but because Kiddy was downright skinny.

She stood in the doorway while her eyes adjusted to the dark. The welcome mat was the same for each unit, only this one was newer than most. A patchwork of colors as if for a circus tent. There was a ratty couch, a coffee table, and a TV, all in a row on the carpet. Each one was draped with a rotting doily like spiderwebs or the thin hair of old women. Otherwise the apartment was the same as hers. Small kitchenette at the far wall, likely the same in that its fridge was empty, its cupboards bare, its sink smelling of stale beer and lime. In the hallway to her right, just beyond the TV, there would be two doors, one on either side.

She stood directly between the doors, listening for the first sound, the faintest gasp, that would disgust her enough to turn around and run. But all there was to hear was a faint rumble, resonant, coming from the door on her left. The door was shut but had no knob and a beam of violet light seemed to burn a hollow through her stomach. She touched the safety-pin where she'd stuck it into the waistband of her panties. She removed it and held it clutched in a fist, then lifted away one finger at a time as if it was something to fear. She knelt before the hole in the door.

A circle. Ceiling and floor were carved out of sight, but central was the waterbed, and atop it lay Rosalina, and atop her lay a small man, small perhaps only in relation, for Rosalina seemed mountainous and fixed and he seemed perched precariously atop her belly, his peaceful face flattened against her bare breasts as if he were high above worry, sleeping. The violet light shone from a lamp set atop a wooden chest, the color filtered out of an enormous pair of panties draped over the shade. They looked magnificent there, glowing, surely not accidental, though seemingly so. Everything seemed this way, a reverent mess, a pristine disarray of undergarments, boas, mirrors angled against the far wall.

Rosalina was sleeping too, but not peacefully. The rumbling belonged to this woman Kiddy had come to sabotage, who seemed less woman and more dormant volcano. A prehistoric incarnation of sex this man came to worship and into which perhaps many had fallen never to be heard touch bottom. And Kiddy backed away from the hole in the door, painfully slow, as if she felt a power there that might seek her out and devour her too.

Standing before the door again, the violet light bore through her stomach before she ran outside with her eyes shut tight, still gripping the safety-pin with her hand upraised to block the sun. She pulled up her shirt, tugged out the waistband of her panties to hide the safety-pin once more, and ran off to see Junie's show.

When Kiddy ran crying past Rosalina's window to the stair no one heard her, though the window was open. The end of summer came in the cool night breeze that had blown the hot afternoon away and now inflated Rosalina's window curtains. Inside that violet room Rosalina was playing hostess to the young man called Spanky.

Spanky woke and rolled off her and stood in a white t-shirt so baggy it appeared a sleeping gown. His ashy knees showed beneath it and it was drawn taut not too far above them. He stood on the balls of his feet like the boxer he was. He rubbed a knuckle across his nose though there was no sweat there.

Rosalina lay in her bed, naked, unmoving.

"Don't try to negotiate, Spanky." She laughed. "Not when you on hard. It's embarrassing, baby."

"I'm just saying I don't know about that bed."

"I know you young, but you can't be scared of a few wet spots."

"The whole goddam bed's a wetspot."

"That's just cause I'm excited about you," she said. With characteristic yet unnatural grace she parted her thighs, let each heavy foot hang off a corner of the bed. "Come on. You never had this much woman."

"I said I'd set you up in Clearwater if you'd kick me down my fifty percent. I got you a place and everything."

"You agreed to forty percent if I gave you an all access VIP pass."

"I was drunk. You're never going to give me that extra ten percent?"

"Hell no. So you can go buy twenty seconds at the campfire with Janine when I done raised the tent? Besides, you got to keep an eye on your product at all times."

"I do have an eye on my product." He looked at her sidelong, squinted an eye shut and let the other travel over her body. It took a long time. "I think that's the problem."

She laughed and her body set a wave rolling beneath her. "Now you know this is where it's at. Everyone does."

He dropped his head, shaking it. He seemed to be considering deeply whatever was said about this woman's magic and what was true and any likely difference between. Finally he raised his head. "Alright."

A few moments later the lamp beside the bed, still covered by the panties, began to rattle. In the violet light no one could have seen the stain bleeding the edges of the bed, which had been bleeding for days, widening by degrees as the carpet soaked the leaking water like a sponge. The waterbed, like most things in Clearwater, like most people, had finally been broken down not by any sabotage, but by the day-to-day.

The next morning Walter Lee was sweeping out the breezeway on the second level of his apartment complex when a noise made him drop the broom and stand dumbstruck. He leaned the broom against the railing. The noise was strange to hear twenty minutes from Long Beach's shore, but that's exactly what it had sounded like, a fierce crashing wave. An old Merchant Marine knew the sound of water. It made him shiver inside his starched chambray workshirt. He'd shaken the confusion from his head long enough to set his cramped hands on the railing and study the debris gathering at the pool's bottom since he'd drained it as the summer's end neared.

It wasn't a matter of weather, of course. This was California. It was a matter of money. Always was. And he was nodding self approval when he heard another noise, just as strange as the first but less sudden, gathering momentum all around him. He felt a hum in the cold railing. He thought of the building what he'd been thinking of the town ever since he'd quit interacting with the people in it: this place is coming apart at the seams.

Then it did, or seemed to. There was a great moaning shudder and the sound raised in pitch until finally with a crash and shock beneath his feet another wave pounded the building and Walter Lee went running stifflegged and straightbacked to Rosalina's apartment. It sounded like a tsunami had hit the corner of the building and he didn't have tsunami insurance, even if there was such a thing.

By now tenants' heads were popping out of doors, taking one look at Walter shambling toward them with only his tired knees to stop him, and ducking back inside one by one on down the line.

Rosalina's door was open, as always, and so was the door to her bedroom. Crying was coming from somewhere but there was nowhere for anyone to stand. The floor had disappeared and in its place there was a giant ragged hole.

On the bottom level, there lay Rosalina, gargantuan even from this superior perspective, half covered in debris on the crushed remnants of her own waterbed and Janine's own bed beneath that.

Janine stepped into view, looked up at Walter who backed away from the edge when a chunk of floor or ceiling either one fell like a stone into a small puddle on Janine's bedroom floor.

"I never wanted nothing bad to happen to her," Janine kept saying. "Mr. Lee?"

"Look at her, Goddangit," Walter Lee said. "She cracked her neck or something. You didn't pull the floor out from under her, did you?"

Janine said, "I bet she's just knocked out."

"Young woman," Walter Lee singsonged. "She looks colder than a witch's tit. Quiet down now. I know you didn't get along and all but a woman falls to her death through her own floor, I'd say it was her time. Look at this Goddang mess. Waterbeds are prohibited. Insurance isn't going to cover this."

It hadn't been only Walter Lee's wife, Kayla Lee, who seemed most responsible for June's flight from Clearwater. Though she had seemed proud to take the responsibility, and she had been the one who'd brought the cops into it.

While Walter spent his time beneath sinks or on his knees wrenching AC units, Kayla spent hers knitting and listening to books on tape. Sometimes sipping from her only china teacup. But generally so enthralled as to let the tea go stagnant, and when the play button popped up, the story over, the knitting done, she set the cup in the sink because the day was done too. Which is all to say that only three things mattered to Kayla Lee: Walter Lee, knitting, and murder mysteries. And not necessarily in that order.

The story playing the day Rosalina died was about a community knitting group who, upon the discovery of a high-end folk-art dealer's body strangled with worsted weight yarn at the local fair, begin their hunt for suspects.

Kayla Lee never even steeped her tea that day.

Her needles clacked and clacked as the old ladies grilled their final suspect, a disillusioned dealer in patchwork quilts, until Rosalina crashed through the second story floor.

Kayla Lee hadn't started. She'd simply set her knitting needles down beside her easychair, turned to the stereo in the bookshelf, looked down her nose at it with her finger hovering, waited for the end of a sentence, and pressed stop.

Kayla Lee only left the house when there was gossip to be heard and spread, and within moments she was out the door and down the stairs and chatting with the first floor tenants. She was far more supple than her husband, despite her pale skin and her nervous demeanor, and so was her imagination.

The ground floor and second story were taped off near the doors of Janine's and Rosalina's apartments. You could hear the cops taking pictures and see an occasional flash. The whole courtyard seemed to have been descended upon by some flock of frantic birds as the police radios chirped and squawked.

Kayla pieced together that Kiddy had left June's room the night before, crying, and that she'd been naked to boot.

Kiddy's mother, Janine, had dabbed her eyes and said, "There's something about that young man that's dangerous."

June was leaning against the second floor railing, looking down on all the commotion. His shirt was off, his chest bore a small square bandage. A cop ducked under the tape behind the two women, but their eyes lingered on June. He did not look away.

"You know Rosalina worked for Spanky?" Kayla said.

"No. She was his?"

"Mmhmm. That's why no one complained about her."

Janine locked eyes with June and said, "Damn. Spanky's gonna make someone pay."

SIX

Spanky's primary assistant, Augustine, now lived in June's old apartment, and was a small time dealer of whatever he could get his hands on. He was not only popular and not just with the opposite sex, but very popular and generally with both. Word was he spent every odd night locked in the house playing Prince or Gap Band much too loud, and opening the door to the occasional customer, which he would do by flinging the door open, standing in the doorway with arms outspread, and yelling, *That's my cheddar!*

Every other night he could be seen spending his meager profits on booze at the Barrel House, dates at the Barrel House, and ending those same nights staggering home from the Barrel House, into the courtyard to sing wanton songs in a jagged falsetto until Walter would yell down for him to shut up. Once he fell asleep on the diving board, his girlish arms and legs suspended out over that bed of young women's hair and the diving board not creaking a bit.

On this particular night, Augustine stumbled out of the Barrel House alone, made a grand bow to the doorman Celli, and began his lurching stumble home, looking like a tango dancer trying to bite the rose free of his invisible partner's mouth.

There was and always had been a semircircle of the buttends of woodplanks arched above the bar's door, so as to look like the end of a wooden barrel. Called the Barrel House for good measure, the owner and bartender and bouncer was a Samoan called Celli because one punch from a fathand meant lights out like a cellar. Not many knew yet that June was back in town, but if asked Celli would have told you he remembered how June's last night at the Barrel House had gone down.

"She can't come in here," he'd told June before they'd even stepped up onto the curb. "She ain't even got shoes."

June looked at her barefeet, her blue toenails. He looked around the parking lot, the guitarcase swinging awkwardly against his knees when he turned side to side. Outside of Starlight liquor vagrants loitered with brown paperbags clutched in their hands or raised to their lips. Cesar's barbershop, next door, was closed, the candycane sign frozen beside the door.

58

"Come on, Celli." June jerked his chin to one side to say *come over to this point of view*. "Ain't no one gonna rat on you, you got the cheapest drinks in Clearwater."

Celli looked around the lot too, then stepped aside with an arm out as if to present them to the folks inside, but once the girl had gone in he laid a heavy hand on June's shoulder and whispered, "Pickin em a little green, don't you think?"

"It ain't like that, man."

"Mmhmm. It never is."

Meanwhile, Augustine made it to the stair unscathed. In the past, he'd been woken up on a neighbor's lawn by sprinklers chirping and spitting at him like urban prairie dogs. But whenever he finally made it home he always stopped and removed his highheeled snakeskin ankleboots—Walter, the landlord, was what one might call *ornery*—and held them flopping against his thigh as he approached his apartment, once again his natural height of five foot one and as he'd say, *don't forget the one half.*

From inside his old apartment, June heard Augustine fumble with the keys a while outside the door, mumble something obscene when the key finally slid into the lock, and stumble inside giggling.

In the dark, Augustine's boots clunked to the floor. When the entryway light came on, Augustine dropped his hand from the switch, slowly, squinting at his packed suitcase, which he hadn't packed, and a few taped up boxes, which he hadn't taped up, occupying the living room floor.

Occupying the couch, with his back against one plush red arm, his dirty ropers kicked up on the other, and a hand that tugged a thin chain hanging near his lit face, was June. Bathed in the strange, greengold, anachronistic light of an ornate vintage lamp hanging from the ceiling—the lampshade looked made of velvet—June had a small cold steel box in his lap. His own TV and stereo on the near wall imposed an at once sentinel and silent noise on the room. Two neatly packed crates of books and movies lounged against each other's odd corners. His guitarcase leaned in the corner with the air of a cocky drunk man assuming he need not find any other place to sleep.

June, for his part, had been waiting for going on two hours now, but seeing Augustine's girlish hipslung stance he didn't think this would last too long.

June said *Hello.*

Augustine barely whispered it, and for the first time, it was a question, "That's my cheddar?"

June didn't know what that meant but he didn't ask either. He wanted to seem as if he knew everything there was to know, and had decided on it all one way or the other. He pointed at the stuff he'd packed for Augustine and left on the floor in the entryway.

He said, "You know what that is?"

Augustine looked at the suitcase, the boxes. "I think so."

"You know what this is?" June knocked the steel box with a knuckle and read its sticker. It said, My Girl Likes To Party All The Time.

Augustine said, "Yeah. I know what that is." His voice was soft and June liked the way he singsonged everything into an insult.

June told Augustine to take a look around. Augustine looked around.

June asked him, "You know what that is?"

Augustine said, "What is it?"

June was biting his bottom lip against a sly smile. "It's where I live. Where do you live now?"

SEVEN

You could see through the only window, speckled now by a few raindrops, the small dark room of the mortuary. Since June was the man in charge of it all he resided over the casket, stood militant and vigil until his mamma knocked at the burnished oak double doors to the mortuary.

He received her small hand in his, escorted her through the sickly yellow lobby, a slender doorway, and down an aisle that ran between two blocks of empty chairs. He led her to precisely the spot he had been standing, at the head of the casket. He put a hand at her waist to show her where to stand. Pressed one to her back to straighten it, cover the how of things. And then he went to the single door of the small, overly furnished room, closed it, and rolled his head around until his neck cracked and he felt ready to stand guard some more.

His watch told him it was seven p.m. He'd had the mortician post eight in the Telegram. The priest was due at seven-fifteen to say the service at seven-thirty, and by eight, when his father's—he smacked his lips at the thought of it, *family*—arrived, they would all be too late.

"He looks good, Junio." His mamma turned and he shifted under her gaze, shook out his feet, tired and hot in his boots. No rest for the wicked. He'd been moving for days and now he felt as if all that kept him awake was momentum. He thought about his mother as someone who no longer belonged to someone else, as someone lonesome and incomplete, and he knew that this was wrong. Not wrong about her, but just wrong to think. She might make another life. She was still pretty in a classic way. His mamma was a small woman with a full figure that narrowed only at the waist and neck, but not much. Once during a party in Uncle Beto's tiny kitchen June's father had called her *zaftig* while sloshing a stein of gourmet beer onto her dress and June like most others had not seemed to know what it meant, though unlike most he had his father's kiltered stacks of books to leaf through later and find it and had used it in a song. But the more he thought about the word he realized it had been used as an insult which no one but his father was meant to uncover and June swore he'd never use words that no one in Clearwater knew the meaning to and when he spoke or wrote songs with the small words he felt like a ventriloquist, he felt filtered or distilled into someone better. So he preferred to hear himself talk or sing over hearing himself think. But he couldn't help thinking as he studied his mamma. She had fiercely thin eyebrows above large dark eyes, and a small round nose above thick dark lips and, much like her features, her expression was a contradiction, one of mourning and resentment both, for his father, whose nose June could see over the wall of the casket like a peak of wax.

"I picked out the suit," June said, pleased.

"The mortuary man dyed his grays, you know. His beard?"

"He was like that before."

"He was like you, Junio. He never knew how good-looking he was back when we was young." She raised a hand to her face and dabbed the corner of her silk scarf to her right eye. Her gaze tracked across the ceiling, as if she were reading her and her ex-husband's shared timeline there. In profile she looked much younger than she was, the dim light quivered on her face, and she seemed caught somehow in a transfiguration, as if memory were not only of the mind but the body too. "He got more conceited as he grew older. Where's Kate?"

"I didn't invite them."

She snapped her head to face him, looked as if he'd just produced a pistol. "No."

"Yeah."

"What are you thinking?"

"They wouldn't have invited us."

"But—"

"They wouldn't have." He checked his watch again. Seven fifteen.

As if he'd orchestrated the whole affair he stood beside the door, his hand upon the doorknob, his shoulder to her in clear dismissal, and there was a knock.

"Mr. Walker?" It was the mortician's contrite sigh of a voice. "It's Father Dover, Sir. He's running late. He was going to walk from the Church but," he paused, gathered his breath, and sighed. "I'm afraid it's begun to rain."

June heard a knock on a door somewhere else in the building. "Excuse me," the mortician said. His voice made him sound small, petite even, but his footsteps betrayed his vast flesh as they reverberated through the walls and the floors as if he and this structure were intertwined. June shuddered to think that maybe each dead body that passed into this place left a little of itself on the mortician's person and it collected and expanded the man outward and he carried it as if it were his own. Maybe this hood owed the mortician a great debt, but if that corpse wrangler got in June's way tonight June wouldn't help to pay it. He might just add more on top.

A door opened somewhere. Murmurs. Then those same heavy steps trod back toward the door against which June now pressed an ear. Other steps, dress shoes and high heels, clacked closer and closer.

"They've came anyways." His mamma stood now with her back against the center of the casket, one foot testing the aisle and the other planted behind her, a finger trailing back to touch the ruffled silk lining. She was trying to choose sides. It didn't take long. She dabbed her eye, and straightened the fall of her dress. "Let them in, mijo."

The doorknob had turned halfway before June gripped it and pressed his shoulder hard against the door.

"Sir?" the mortician said. "Sir, other guests have arrived."

June mumbled, "They're not guests."

"Excuse me, sir?"

"Guests gotta be welcome and these ain't welcome. Send them out."

"But. Sir?" The mortician seemed to abandon his constant sorrow for a panic betrayed by his fat man's manner of breathing shallow, wet, and nasal.

"Interlopers," June hissed. "Send them out."

The knob was turned once more but June had both hands on it by then. A younger version of him had been chased out of town and he wouldn't have that again. They would have new things about him to remember, new stories to tell. He pressed all his weight against the door, gripping the doorknob like he was about to lift a sledgehammer up to bring down on all their heads.

The giant could probably crash in on him if he wanted, but June had faith in the man's sense of decorum, else he'd have at least cussed him by now.

"Junie, you let us in," his father's brother-in-law called through.

His step-mom said, "Junie, you let me see my husband."

June laughed. "Ain't your husband anymore, Kate. Til death do you part. Can't read that more ways than one."

His mamma moved then. She slid across the length of the aisle and was already striking him about the head and face, barehanded one and purse in the other, until the trinkets inside poured out over his head and she backed away and chucked the limp leather thing in his face. "I'm ashamed of you."

He'd taken it all stonefaced but now he corkscrewed his tongue against the inside of his molars and glared at her until he saw her through slits. He stared through her, or ceased seeing her, imagined he had opaque lids that dropped before any pain could show.

"Don't lie to me, mamma," he told her, calm, inflectionless. "They wouldn't have let us see him. Don't be fooled."

Then there was a pounding on the door and he realized he'd loosened his grip on the doorknob. Wouldn't even consider leaving his post to get a chair to prop beneath it.

The priest's voice came muffled through the door, "Junie Jiminez, it's Father Dover. Now, I know you are in mourning," he slapped the door a few times, "but you have got to let us inside of there."

"You can come on in, Father."

"All of us."

"Can't do it."

It was quiet. He heard the rain pinging off a duct in the building, a leak somewhere. Thunder. He looked toward the casket as if to garner an approving nod from the man inside. A strobic flash of lightning stuttered his vision of the casket, his mother, his hand clawed round the doorknob.

"Alright now, Junie. We're not gonna break down the door. Why don't you let me in, son? Let me talk to you, okay?"

"Of course, Father. Make everyone back off."

He listened while the priest shooed them away. When he was satisfied he opened the door, leaning out as if he were mounted to it, "Good evening, Father. Thanks for coming."

The priest's black garment seemed to draw color and light off his face, and the women's too where they stood behind him. The mortician loomed out of focus behind them all. They looked like undead guests at a funeral for their own kind, a reversal of ceremonies where a dead priest received rather than bid farewell. The other man, his father's brother-in-law, stood apart, wore chino slacks and deck shoes. His shirt was patterned with bottles of beer.

June grinned at the man. "Nice outfit."

The man laughed and reduced his chin to a few folds of flesh. "You're unbelievable, bastard."

The priest raised a steady white hand. Cold radiated from it. "Now."

June hawked and spat and a waxy globe arced past the priest's upraised hand, the women's horrified faces, and down onto the toe of the man's left deckshoe.

The man studied his shoes.

The mortician just sighed, shook his head side to side, above them all in a manner and weight almost bovine.

June called them all interlopers and took the priest by

the elbow. Before anyone else could move he had the priest inside and was leaning his back against the closed door. He swiped a forearm across his mouth, grinning, the mustache on his lip thinning out when he did so, making the grin more ragged, wolfish.

Someone was pounding on the door now, not just knocking, but trying to knock it off its hinges. *Good thing it ain't that giant,* June thought. *Or I'd be smithereens.*

"This is low, Junie," the priest was saying. "Dirty, scandalous, and low."

But June "Junie" Walker was known for this sort of behavior. Rightfully or no.

At that knowledge, he bared his teeth now, speaking against the mortuary's door. "It's low, and I'll go to confession for it. I will. I feel bad about embarrassing mamma." The door rumbled at his back. "Handling you rough, too. I'll confess all that."

His mamma was pushing at her cheeks with her fingertips. She adjusted her dress. "Hello, Father. Thank you for coming."

The priest nodded solemnly and a shard of light swept up then down his bald head. He looked at her and at June and at her again, said, "My condolences."

The mortician was wheezing between shouts for the family to leave off the door. They only pounded harder,

70

and June could feel it through his back straight on into his chest. As if they were taking hammers to his ribcage, his sternum. "Better get going with the services, Father. Don't think I can hold out all night."

The priest looked at him for a long while before he said, "I won't do it. Not like this."

June didn't want to order the priest around or disrespect him. Didn't want this whole thing to stink of some sin. It wasn't a matter of religion at all. What it was was a matter of principle.

"It's words, Father. That's all it is."

"Then you say them."

"You know I can't do that. You just say those words and we all go home to bed."

June felt the door open if only an inch and it clipped his heels and he felt himself almost knocked down onto his face. "Goddang. Think they just threw the fat man at me. They'd do it too. They tried to have my pops buried out there in Flagstaff when he lived his whole life here. Only way I got to see him was cause I offered to pay for the services." He began to laugh. "Every penny. Soon as he died they took a trip to Sedona on his insurance money. You know what they were gonna bury him in? A cardboard box." He turned his mouth to the door so that he was nearly kissing it and shouted, "A shoebox!"

"I'll not perform the services."

His mamma walked down the center aisle to take the front right seat.

"It's all set up, Father. You just have to talk and a man goes to heaven. "

They both looked at his mother's silhouette where she sat facing the casket, her head wobbling atop her shoulders like an off-balance urn.

The priest looked upward, pained, inquisitive, as if he believed that this were his own divine test. His mouth was open, his jaw muscles tight, his eyes frenetic and unfocused. The pounding at the door continued. The thunder grew louder until the sky seemed to be tumbling onto the rooftop.

June looked away so the priest could think alone. Outside the room's only window rain was falling in sheets that hung from the streetlamps. As a teenager he'd seen it like this a few winters and he'd run to the garage for his father's raft. His mamma had told him no but there was no father to have to ask for permission. He knew like those old days the poor sewers would clog. The slick city streets would run like rivers.

The pounding at the door ceased. Footsteps took the hum of life further and further from the door. June smiled. The interlopers would catch hell hauling their asses back to LAX in all this mess. When he heard the priest begin to mumble the service June shut his eyes and made the sign of the cross. He said in his head, *I know it's been a long time, but thanks anyway for the rain.*

EIGHT

Brenton said:

When I chaperoned a dude out to the mortuary the next day, Sam told me Junie and the Priest and the moms and the dead pops was in there for hours, after even the family had jetted, and he knew they was in there cause he could feel it, other living people, like a hum, but it was quiet as when he's all alone with the dead in that place at night. Only sounds of the storm, Sam said. Said he was freaked, and Sam's used to freaky shit. I sure as hell ain't. I told him as much and he bent down and sniffed my breath and when he backed away I could still smell his tres flores hair grease.

"Have you been drinking?" he asked me.

I told him he just smelled my morning coffee, which wasn't no lie cause I take my morning coffee with rum in it.

I told him I had to get going cause Mary and I were gonna get lunch together, we been talking more each day. But he wouldn't let me leave.

I ain't one for gossip, and besides I was pissed at Junie and didn't really care what kind of trouble he was getting into, but Sam stood at the back door with a hand on my shoulder that weighed a ton. So I couldn't really go anywhere, could I?

Sam said, after trying to decide if he should go in and see if he didn't have more customers—like they's all killed each other, I mean—the priest came out, pale, sweaty, smacking his tongue to the roof of his mouth like he was thirsty.

Between Sam and Walter's wife and all the chismosas around town, you know shit get around. Two stories came out of that night.

One, Junie forced the priest to perform a funeral against his will, at what threat no one knew but plenty imagined.

Two, Junie let his pops be buried without a funeral in the end cause the priest wouldn't give in. Buried his pops without a true funeral just to prove a point.

There was other stories in between, like the priest felt bad for Junie, or Junie was right to do what he done, but those ones weren't as popular.

Me, I went back and forth about what I believed.

Like that day, after Sam told me about Junie's last stand, and after my lunch date with Mary, I had to pick this dead dude up out a ditch. He'd been hit on that loop that comes off the 710 freeway heading east out of Compton. Dude had been knocked clear into the bushes and not a what the hell about it. Just a few cops and EMTs shooting the shit like he wasn't there, making jokes about how his chest and face picked the roadstripes up off the asphalt like his faceskin was made of silly putty.

So I was chaperoning him back to the morgue, sipping on a strong, and I mean strong, cup of coffee. "You want some?"

Dude didn't drink.

So I asked him did he know Junie's pops. Maybe he could find out the true story. Maybe they're worse gossips in heaven. Maybe all they talk about is us. Course I'm just playing, you know? I don't really think they can hear me. Wouldn't wish they could.

What I do wish is that Junie'd just stayed being my friend. Wish he'd told me all these things himself. If I'd still been knowing him like a friend, like a good friend, I could stop making him up in my head second hand. Stop picking the stories one by one off the grapevine. Stop picking them up from where I found them, facedown in the street.

NINE

Spanky watched in the mirror as the razor cut a swatch of face out of the froth on his cheek. He could see Kiddy over his shoulder, tiny, lying in bed.

"Why won't you take us?" she asked. "It's just a little movie shoot and it ain't even that far."

"Right now we have a deal. I do things for you and you do things for me and it's a private deal and I like it that way. You go out to L.A., you meet new people, you make new deals, and then you cut out on old ones."

She sat up in bed and he leaned in closer to the mirror with his chin pointed high and the razor aloft. She said, "I could be meeting people right here in Clearwater, you know?"

He looked down his nose at her reflection, and pointed at it with the foamy razor. "Yeah. You could be meeting them. But you ain't dealing with them." He tapped the razor in the sink. Done that quick; there wasn't much to shave around his fat mustache. He took a towel from where he'd tucked it into the waist of his old boxing shorts and pressed his face into the towel. When he dropped the towel she was standing naked right behind him like an apparition. He was slight, but muscled. She was slight, and fine-lined. He wove by her like an opponent entering on the wrong side of the ring.

Outside he went from kennel to kennel, dog to dog, and Kiddy trailed behind. He reached down into a bloody bucket full of sirloin and set a slab at a kennel door. He opened the door with one hand and ran the opposite hand back over the dog's coat while it chomped away. In the other hand he'd been palming a syringe. "They know the hand that feeds them, and the hand that stabs them too. They're smarter than you think." When the dog was bloodymuzzled and ignorant of anything but the raw meat—he kept them hungry for this purpose—he squeezed what flesh there was on the stonemuscled dog he called Potsy into a small fold at its rear, and raised the syringe before his eye to watch its tip bead fluid.

Kiddy stood behind him, seemingly still an apparition to him, and a boring one at that. "I ain't one of your dogs, Spanky."

"And this ain't a audition." He turned to her, had to slouch to see her eye to eye, and brought the bloodygloved hand up to her chin to help it up.

"You can't cage me."

"You sound stupid."

Her nostrils flared when she rolled her eyes down to see the gelid matter at the tip of his accusing finger. She swallowed something that soured her face. "I'm over this."

He ignored her, seeming cool as he thumbed the plunger down, tugged the needle free, slammed the door—this was the only moment that might have betrayed any anger had Kiddy not been distracted by the anger he'd welled up within her with his disinterest in her career and seeming disinterest in her breakup speech.

Spanky went to the next cage, wiping the glove clean on the butcher's apron, leaving a red Rorschach on his chest, the only tool for Kiddy to study in interpreting their discussion. Pockets ran up and down the apron's front like a half-stitched quilt, and in each pocket there was a collection of plastic wrapped vials which he fingered through intensely and blindly and gently as a piano player, all the while raking his bottom teeth down his mustache. He removed a plastic blister pack from a pocket, thumbed the vial through the thin foil backing. "I need your help with this one."

"You know I don't like your dogs."

"But you would if I drove you to L.A.?"

"It wouldn't hurt."

"You keep putting up with me. What do you see? Who knows? No one knows about Kiddy. But she keeps putting up with me."

When she turned to take the steak from the bucket he stroked her hair and wrapped an arm around her, cradling her head in the hollow of his shoulder. They both stared down at the syringe in their cupped hands like a proposal.

"You know what's in here?" he asked.

She shook her head. She forced a smile but it looked more like a gnashing of teeth.

"The good dogs, the ones that do everything right, the ones that work day after day, they get steroids, vitamins, they get painkillers. The other ones, the ones that get forgotten, left behind, the losers, get something that makes their hearts swell," he touched the needle to his fingertip. "Until—" His face was close now. His lips on her neck. He drew her flesh between his teeth and sucked, pulled away and put his lips to her ear. He whispered, "The heart goes boom."

Already the part of her neck that he'd bitten was turning a mottled purple. "Can I put my initials?" he asked. "Like teenagers?" He made a whining sound like a dog. After a time she began to smile, but when she wiped the sweaty bangs off her face her hand shook. "I didn't think it was that hot out here," he said, "you feeling okay?"

He went to the bucket for a slab of steak and opened the next door and tossed it in. He injected the dog without switching needles. "Just vitamins, baby," he said, to her or the dog either one. The dog whined then started in gnawing on the meat.

"I'm going home," she said.

"Let me get cleaned up." He jogged over to a towel hanging with a jump-rope on a hook in the garage. "You shouldn't have to walk."

June was watching her from the breezeway above when she got back home.

The Vietnamese couple in 4B had their faces pressed to the glass for an instant before they dropped the blinds. June had moved into 3B right next door, and already his neighbors seemed the contradictory combination of nosy and reclusive.

81

Kiddy hadn't even glanced back at Spanky's car. She strutted her way across the street, highheels clicking when she got to the paving stones, hammering once she got into the courtyard, a steady rhythm June began to hum along to before he said, "Who was that?"

She looked up but June knew he was out of her line of sight. He was leaning against the railing straight above her. There was a stark white part across the front of her scalp for the bangs that fanned outward and up. The toes of her highheels were sharp triangles sticking out of her shoulders.

"Up here," he called. "Who was that?"

"Who's asking?" She looked up, finally locked onto him.

"You know who."

"You know who-who?" She walked around the pool's edge to her door near the corner stair.

He hesitated. "You know who you want taxi-ing you around and it ain't whoever that was." June kept his voice casual by force of will and clamped jaws.

"I wouldn't mess with Spanky. You and him are grown now."

"And don't some of us grow too fast?"

She turned, smiled, raised her key to the doorknob. "Where you been at, anyway?"

"Alone."

She smacked her lips. "I said 'where,' not 'what.'"

He asked where she'd been and she said right here. He said he knew that and she went on inside. He could hear her mother Janine's voice echo through the courtyard, asking who she'd been talking to. Kiddy had said nobody and he hadn't missed it. It gave him pause as he walked the breezeway to his door.

Kiddy called out to him and he slammed his brakes, turned right round to rest his elbows on the railing as if he'd been there coolly smoking his cigarette the whole time, for all time, perhaps til time just quit.

"Yeah?" he mumbled, the cigarette rising on his lips.

She'd stuck just her head out the door. She was smiling. "I guess you can go on inside like you were. I didn't mean to startle you."

He chucked the cigarette into the pool below. "What do you want?"

"You think you could take me and Daisy out to L.A.? We got this shoot. I asked Spanky but he don't want to do it. He thinks I'm gonna meet some hipster and leave him in the dust." She swept a stray strand of hair behind her ear, only to have it fall across her temple again. Her eyes lingered on him for a long time, and it was the first time, and heat washed down his back so all parts of him went soft but one and he leaned harder on his elbows and backed his hips off the railing. "Do I look like a hipster?"

"To him?"

"To you."

"So you'll drive?"

TEN

Walter said:

But anyway now that Junie'd come back that girl started hanging round him like a kitten round a scratching post. I could have told you that would happen. I could have told you what happened next, too. Course she had that other man. Course he wasn't any good, not that Junie was but Junie wasn't bad either, he was just kind of a character. And of course she was playing them both like pianos. Like the ones that play themselves even.

I could see her sometimes in my dreams. Her sitting on that diving board of a day, creaking its complaints, men going toe to toe in that empty pool beneath her. Her cutting her own hair all day and night like in some old myth, like some old goddess, always more and more hair draped down and cradled in her lap to cut, and it all falling into that poolbed.

My back creaking its own complaints and more hair falling for me to clean up out of there. And men bound to fall too. And ain't no one who could clean that up.

ELEVEN

They exited the freeway at Sepulveda, Kiddy and Daisy saying June'd never get them to the shoot in time, and afternoon gridlock as far as June could see. He didn't like the look of that steel wall and felt it a challenge placed to see was he the man who could part it, or leap over it like so many nights walking walls as a young man, staying out just to see the sun rise. June shot left in front of a gastruck and the driver laid on the horn, but June had already swung the tiny Kharmann Ghia across opposing traffic, to the sound of still more honking, and cut down a sidestreet.

Kiddy laughed. "Little hoopdy can fly."

June revved the engine and it sounded like a lawnmower caught in too-tall grass. He laughed at it his damn self. He'd never been one to care much about cars and if the motor needed work he'd do no more than raise the hood and chuck a screwdriver at it. Kick a tire and call it good.

Daisy said, "Why's the interior all ripped up?" She reached up and touched the black felt sagging from the ceiling. When she touched the side of the passenger seat in front of her a coilspring popped through the leather.

June tuned the stereo away from the latest pop hit. "The cops," he said, and settled on an oldies station.

He looked at Daisy in the rearview mirror. Her eyebrows and mole were drawn on dark, the mole on the right cheek this time, and a little higher on her face. Daisy plucked up from the floorboards a tattered Audobon bird-watcher's guide. "The cops?"

Kiddy turned to Daisy. "He didn't always look so nerdy. He used to dress normal."

Daisy said, "I think he looks cute."

Art Laboe was on the radio making a dedication. From Silas to Lola, our song por vida. Hey There Lonely Girl. The girls laughed at the old man's nasal DJ voice dedicating songs for *rucas* and *novios* and *sanchas* and *cholos*. June cranked down his window, a workout, and he wiped his forehead both at that and the chore of driving through traffic. "What's this audition for again?" He plucked the cigarette from his lips and let his arm hang out, the hot winds of downtown stoking the cigarette scissored in his fingers.

Daisy said, "It's an arthouse piece. Smart shit. Real acting."

"Listen to you—" Kiddy paused. Kiddy had faced forward and said it as if it were something to spit out the window. "—Linda. Some stuckup college kids put it together. It'll get us bigger parts at least."

"Daisy Columbine when we get there, bitch. Got it? Daisy Columbine."

"What's the thing called?" June looked at Kiddy, turned down the radio gone to a commercial for collision attorney Larry H. Parker, *I'll fight for you.* He smirked at her.

Kiddy said, "Don't look at me like that."

"Like what?" He knew Kiddy was a pile of kindling, but he couldn't get her started no matter how hard he slammed the flint to stone. He baited her with a laugh and said, "You don't seem in too good a mood. You even want to do this?"

She looked at him with her chin raised and he could see where the white face powder met her skin like a mask. She batted her heavy eyelashes once, twice.

"Just saying." He shrugged. "Don't seem like it to me."

Daisy held up a blue flyer with some writing and a picture of an egg Xeroxed onto it. *"The Story of the Eye."*

June and Kiddy both said, "Never heard of it." Daisy giggled and June turned a sharp left. The orange afternoon sun was a torch on the hood's crest. June put his hand on Kiddy's and she pulled it away, so he tried feebly to disguise his intent, and swatted the visor down.

It broke loose and slapped to the dash. "Fucking cops," he said.

It was a small house in Silver Lake. Not unusual. Looked pricey. Tucked behind an oak, a cactus, palm trees near large ferns, in the usual manner of Californians who cannot make decisions in a garden where everything grows. The kind of place with owners that wouldn't want a broken sun-visor frisbeed onto its street, which happened anyway.

The Ghia's small motor idled at random in the small cul de sac, shot dark smoke from the exhaust at the girls who, before realizing the trunk was up front, had opened the rear hatch to get their clothes and found only the engine.

"Forgot," Kiddy said.

June was smiling to himself in the side-view mirror, and she let him smack her rump when she passed close. Though, she wouldn't look at him and she kept her head high and her back stiff, and afterward he felt cheap and double-crossed, like an alcoholic trusted not to drink the last of the beer. She waited for Daisy to open the front hatch. They took out plastic grocery bags stuffed with multicolored bundles of clothes.

"Pick us up in a few hours?" Kiddy struck a pose with a thumb jammed into her jeans to show her belly to him.

"I'll go grab a bite."

Not fifteen minutes later he was dinged in at a diner near Olvera Street eating a slice of pumpkin pie between sips of coffee. He smacked his lips between bites. The pumpkin was from a can but it was good and spicy. He'd brought that blue flyer inside to check out and as he was reading it he forgot to blow on his coffee—forgot to stop drinking too—and the coffee scorched his mouth. The clinking of spoons and ceramics ceased, and June thought of crickets' chirps stalling when there's danger in the forest and, though it was bright hot outside the diner's window, his face went suddenly grey. He felt as if a cloud had swept overhead and rain was coming just for him. He scanned the flyer faster and faster.

He set the mug down, breathing fast through his teeth, kicked back his chair and bowled over the man behind him. He apologized and ran out the door with a ding.

His chair sat askance, his flannel jacket hanging from it.

The man got down to his knees and seemed to be trying to salvage his Key Lime, or what hadn't been smeared onto the black and white tile. The diner was silent. Cups floated near lips but didn't touch them. Hands holding knives froze over their steaks. It all seemed the wake of an earthquake, awaiting the come of the aftershock.

When June crashed back through the entrance no on had yet moved and everyone sucked in a deep sudden breath at the sight of him as if this all were a reversal of events just passed. The man spooning the Key Lime off the floor covered his head with both hands.

June scanned the frightened faces in the room.

Mostly old folks.

He went to the chair and yanked his jacket from it and ran off.

The flyer sat where he'd left it, soaking up spilled coffee on the table.

THE STORY OF THE EYE: AN ADAPTATION OF THE MOST DISTINGUISHED EROTIC TALE EVER TO EXAMINE THE OUTER LIMITS OF THE SEXUALLY DEVIANT.

TWELVE

Daisy sat naked on a toilet full of hardboiled eggs—shelled, glossy, bobbing like drowned mens' skulls.

The bathroom was cramped, just a few feet square, but still the boom man, the cameraman, and the director all occupied the doorway.

The director was a young man in a ratty t-shirt and he looked like he'd shaved with a cheesegrater. The boom man wouldn't take his eyes off her breasts. The cameraman never quit crouching behind the camera, grimacing, his eye pressed to it, lenses and focus rings spinning of their own accord like some botched experiment to fuse man to machine.

Daisy had her arms wrapped round the folds of her belly, out of nausea or shame you couldn't tell.

"You really stepped it up, Daisy," the director said, scratching his stubble. It sounded like sandpaper. "You're better for this part anyway. You're a natural. Now you take up one of those eggs. Watch them. They're slippery. Not to worry about germs," he said, nodding to a bottle of bleach in the bathtub. "We took care of that."

Daisy opened her thighs and stared down between them. The eggs never ceased their jostling.

The director went on. "You read the script, right?"

"Yeah I read it."

"So you reach in and take up an egg and do like it says in the script on action. Now, one, two, three, action!"

Daisy looked up at the ceiling but the boom mic loomed overhead, long, dark, and furry. So she closed her eyes. She reached her hand between her legs and brought up a shelled hardboiled egg. White, glossy, like an eye.

The camera man zoomed in on her lowering the egg to the triangle of hair between her thighs.

The camera whined and zipped like the machinations of all minds crammed into that room.

Then something crashed into the house.

Daisy dropped the egg with a plop and opened her eyes.

The director stepped out of the doorway, back into the hall. He was rubbing his chin. "What the hell? Hey man, you can't be in here." He took a cellphone from his pocket and pointed it like a gun. "I'll call the cops."

The cellphone was slapped from his hand and crashed into the wall and split into two pieces. The battery spun on the floor. He was backhanded across his nose and he crumpled to the floor with a nasal, "Oh Jesus."

A boot kicked the cameraman's back and he tumbled onto his stomach and the camera smashed onto the tiles. Daisy watched as man and machine went their separate ways at her feet. She screamed. Looked up.

The boom man retreated, wielding the boom like a lance, out of sight. Daisy watched as June crossed the open door, the sleeves of his flannel rolled back. He returned to stand in the doorway and look at her.

"Put some godforsaken clothes on." June looked down at the director, where he sat back flat to the wall and legs flopped forward. "Porno with good dialogue is still just porno."

The director spoke through bloody cupped hands, "It's fucking art." He shouted, "Fascist."

June stepped out of the doorway and out of Daisy's smiling sight.

June found the boom man in a living room filled with bean-bag chairs. There was a light square on the carpet where a TV had been. Boxes filled the hall. But a tacky goldgilt glass coffeetable with coke laid out in five short lines occupied the center of the room.

"L fucking A," June said. "Where is she?"

"She's in the bathroom."

"Not her."

"She's not here. She wouldn't do the scene." He pulled a beanie off of his head and his wispy hair made the shape of a flame. He tossed the beanie aside and braced the mic as if for battle.

June was proud of Kiddy for a moment, but the moment didn't last. He realized he didn't think highly enough of Kiddy anymore to believe the boom man, and besides she seemed to have become the kind of person who would turn this sort of thing down out of power, not any moral qualms. But then again he didn't know who she'd become. Ten years gone.

June mockcharged the boom man, now swinging too wide, dropped into a crouch, just before the mic cut the coffeetable clean in goldgilt halves. Each half toppled to the floor and shattered.

The boom man said, "Shit."

The director whined from the hallway, "That's my grandma's coffeetable."

By then June'd wrested the mic from the boom man. He raised it once as if to strike and the boom man cowered. "She left," he said behind fanned hands. "She said she was taking a bus to the metro."

"Daisy," June called.

"Yeah?" Her voice echoed from the bathroom.

"Got your clothes?"

"Not yet."

"Well let's get them and let's get the hell out of here."

"Sure," she called. "Junie?"

"Uh huh?"

"You think you could pull the cameraman out of my way? He hasn't moved once."

"Oh." He smiled. He could be proud of himself, if not Kiddy. "Coming."

Just before dark they pulled up to the bus stop bench where Kiddy sat bouncing one leg over the knee of the other. You could see clear up to the inside of her thigh. She sat before a backlit ad on the wind shelter asking people to spay and neuter their pets. Daisy cranked on the handle to roll the window down.

June called, still looking at her thigh, "Hey, Gilda, you need a ride?"

Kiddy looked through Daisy as if she weren't in the passenger seat or even in the world and said, "Who?"

"Gilda. You know, Hayworth?"

"No." She touched two fingers to the back of each earlobe and her hoopearings bobbed. They were tugging her lobes down and the piercing was a slit. She took them out.

June put the car in park and the engine reached its idle at a higher pitch than usual. It no longer sounded like a lawnmower stuck in tall grass. It sounded more like one flipped upside down.

Daisy whispered, "She's just embarrassed. She gets like this when she's embarrassed." Daisy's mole was missing from the cheek facing him. Maybe she'd moved it to the other one.

Anyway, he had to believe what she told him about Kiddy. He didn't know how Kiddy got, anymore. He felt like he didn't know how anyone got but himself and that was easy enough: angry. June saw Daisy as someone who had a talent he lacked—in the dim streetlight coming through the windshield she could still see clearly what Kiddy was feeling. He looked at Kiddy. Her face was set as she watched passing traffic. Trying to seem indifferent, he figured.

"Come on," he called past Daisy. "You won't get home for hours."

97

A bus's headlights washed into the car and turned his threat to milk. He smacked the steering wheel. The bus behind them honked and Kiddy uncrossed her leg and leaned forward without leaving the bench. She used whatever acting skill she possessed to seem seriously intent on the bus's arrival.

"Look it," June said. "I'm glad you left that house."

Kiddy said, "I know. You got a grin on your face I'd have to slap to knock off."

"You really never seen the movie Gilda?" he asked.

It was silent for a long time. The comparison to Gilda shouldn't have bothered Kiddy if she hadn't seen the movie. Even if she had, at least Gilda was a powerful woman. He didn't know why, or how, but she was. Then again, he hadn't seen it in years. Maybe he only remembered her that way. Maybe Kiddy wasn't his Gilda at all. June was looking at Kiddy, waiting, feeling like some magic property inherent in the sound of her voice was the only thing that would get them all moving forward again.

"Maybe," she said.

"Maybe isn't an answer. You've seen it or you haven't. Like you've listened to music in the last ten years or you haven't. It's a simple yes or no to a simple question."

The bus honked again.

"Yes."

"Did you like it?"

"Yes."

"It's showing this month at Rosecrans. Do you want to go see it with me tonight?"

Kiddy stood and faced the bus.

Daisy got out and pushed the seatback forward and got in the back. When Kiddy got in, Daisy put a hand on each of the seats and leaned forward until her face was between them. "It's a real good movie." Daisy retreated into the dark of the backseat, her hands still on the seat-backs, fingers thrumming. After a long while Daisy said, "Can we all just pretend that today didn't happen?"

June put the car into gear, pulled away. "Fine by me."

But as they rose up the freeway onramp Kiddy answered. So much time had passed that it seemed a new conversation altogether, seemed something she'd been wanting to bring up herself, and June blinked at her words. "Maybe I'll see it with you tomorrow."

He told her fine, and checked the traffic over his right shoulder as he merged. Fine by him.

THIRTEEN

But she didn't see the movie with June the next night. Or the night after that. Most nights she wasn't even home to be picked up for a date and most everybody said she was at Spanky's. Spanky kept her in fancy highheels and hoop earrings. He kept her in hoochie tops that were made of better material than the ones the other girls bought at the little chinito store, on sale, two-for-fifteen. Mornings her and Daisy still sat that diving board though; industry standard seemed a goal unattainable and if at all, achieved only through determination, swapmeet bought salon scissors, and hours upon hours of free time.

June could wait her out until the next fire season. He had the apartment paid through until summer. Wads of cash in his guitar. Reach inside once and there was food, laundry, and whiskey for a month. Wait and watch and hope Kiddy's fire took.

He was around the apartment enough to help Walter with what he could. He thought Phillips was a brand of screwdriver, so it wasn't much. Help carry an A/C unit up the stairs. Help rip out the carpet and lay a new one. Walter had him in his apartment for beers in the afternoon, Kayla hiding in the bedroom. June had Walter over for more beers and to watch old movies in the evenings, no one hiding, no one to hide, and little in June's apartment to prove anyone lived there at all. Just some movies and books still in boxes. A guitar and its case. A stereo. The TV.

Kayla never seemed to leave their place, but somehow she was Walter's, and so June's, connection to the city. He heard through her that Spanky had arranged it so Kiddy only had to stroll into Nina's on Alondra Boulevard and the two Vietnamese women who owned that shop would mangle the English language in a contest to be the one to compliment Kiddy first. One would turn the blinds closed so the room only glowed, stuffy, damp even with the fans on, from all the towelfaced women's wet hair left to soak in sinks while the women waited silent as urban mummies and the shopowners tended to Kiddy.

She'd prop her two small feet on that stool that, like déjà vu, had until that moment been a few feet away, and she'd say, *Blue.* And they'd set to scrubbing, and rubbing, and scraping her feet until the soles looked permeable as cream. Then they set to work painting her toenails blue, each woman chatting at her glottally, and each tending a single foot. That was all until June took to sitting on that diving board each night and crooning. Then Kiddy was seen less and less around town.

After almost a month, June began to figure that maybe Kiddy was considering him. Why else would he let his voice get more brazen and full and expressive each night? Why else would he call out the number of showings left to go see the movie she'd promised him?

June sat on that diving board, it creaking pained rhythms of the soul music, the rhythm and blues music, the just-a-few-shows-left-come-on-Kiddy blues music, singing it up through the courtyard, at the night.

FOURTEEN

Walter said:

I'd left the Barrel House a drink or two in, and feeling a year or two younger, my back a little more limber. When I got inside the courtyard I ripped some brown leaves off the potted plant near the door. I wanted to get the broom and went to the utility closet next to the entryway; we didn't want it right out there front of god and the world too. But I stopped, because there was Junie sitting on the edge of that rickety old diving board.

His feet were dangling down into the empty space of the pool. He had his hands round a tall bottle of whiskey, and his head was hanging over it, and he was snoring. He tilted forward and the board creaked loud and the bottle tilted a bit too. Whiskey started pouring out in splashes, and each time he seemed near about to wake up, but then he'd sink further forward. Then the whiskey poured, steady streaming on out the bottle's mouth to make a sizzling sound on the poolbed. Soon the bottle'd slipped out his hands, seemed to fall in the moonlight forever, silvery, twisting, me so nervous about the crash coming and when it came Junie started up straightbacked. Kiddy sat in her window as usual, cut head to toe down the middle by the moonlight.

Junie looked up at me, eyes red as hell, but smiling. In all the commotion my nerves had tightened my back right up again, felt like I'd been horsebit and the horse had never let go.

"Hi, Mr. Lee," Junie said. He stood, barely, tottering on that board. "Hi Kiddy," he said, but he wasn't even looking at her.

"Hey," she said.

Then he sang real soulful, "Tomorrow night's . . . the last night we got . . .

to see that same old show. Baby, I don't hear 'no,' so save your breath, lest you say . . .

lest you say you'll go."

Kiddy said, "You just make that up?"

"Just now." He looked up at the sky.

I did too. There weren't any stars out to see. The city glow reflected off the dark so the sky shone like marble.

Kiddy asked him, "For me?"

"Nope. For Walter Lee." He spun round to face me. "Well, Walter, what's it gonna be? You going to that show? Last night to see old Rita Hayworth."

I couldn't help but laugh. "Not allowed. My Kayla don't like me to see no woman but her. Not even in the movies."

Junie said, "Guess I got an extra ticket." He spun around to face Kiddy, him on that board, her in that window, both of them surrounded by nothing, on top of nothing, wasting time for nothing.

She said, "Pick me up just before dark?"

He did a leftface and the diving board groaned deeper than usual and I called, "Careful on that," but he'd already hopped off the board and was in the dark of the stairwell.

"Careful," he said to himself and it echoed out to me as he stepped up the stair. I watched him walk across the breezeway and go inside. I watched Kiddy watch him and then wave at me and drop the blinds.

Careful, I said again. Then I went on up to Kayla.

FIFTEEN

June had a blanket over his shoulder, a flask weighing down the chestpocket of his flannel, and a smile on his face when he knocked on Kiddy's door. The air around him was cool and blue, as if the sky had collapsed into the courtyard. White clouds capped the complex and the courtyard hummed electric.

Walter was upstairs sweeping the breezeway, but June tried not to think about work. The season for that would come. Janine opened the door, propped an elbow on the doorframe, and slunk her shoulder expertly loose of her halter-top's strap.

"Oh. Hey, Junie."

He stopped smiling. There were a lot of women Kiddy could grow up to be like. This was the one he couldn't stand.

In her presence he became again that selfsame creature of solid flesh and prominent bone he'd seemed on the day of his false accusation. His face grim as the skull beneath it, the skull you could see clearly at the jaw and cheeks, strangely beautiful if only for the constant assertion of mortality, the beauty of things that are fleeting. She seemed to transform him by some magic gaze, the opposite of which Kiddy held.

"Where you been at?" she asked.

"Went to visit my daddy." June wouldn't look at her, choosing to look at the tarnished home of the deadbolt in the doorframe instead, and she thumbed the loose strap of her shirt back up and then he did look. "I'd like to take Kiddy out if that's okay with you, ma'am."

"It okay with her? It okay with Spanky? I know him better than you did. I don't think he'd like that."

He shut his eyes. This was a test. Kiddy's origins, Kiddy herself, that man Spanky, this city's idea of him: all things he wanted changed and not all of them changeable. He was reading a long list scribbled on the backs of his eyelids trying to figure out how he would know when he was done.

He opened his eyes, smirked. "I'll have to remember to have a talk with Spanky sometime soon."

Kiddy knocked Janine's elbow out of the way when she burst out over the threshold. She began pulling June out of the courtyard and Janine shut the door on them and on the shushing sound of Walter's broom in the breezeway.

Walter kept sweeping. After a while the Vietnamese couple from 4B left their apartment and descended the northeast stair to head out back. Brenton staggered into the court-yard just as they left, as if by some haunting the building could sustain only a certain number of tenants, their stories, and flung them out of doors as needed and sucked new ones inside as it saw fit. Walter stopped sweeping. He fumbled with the collar of his chambray work shirt to button the topmost button but he still seemed like he was just stalling out, being nosy.

Down below, Brenton fumbled with then dropped his keys with a rattle. He took a drink from the brownbagged bottle he held in one hand, and bent down, reaching shakily for the keys with the other. After a while he seemed to forget that he'd been wanting to pick something up and decided instead on putting himself down, twisting his legs round each other to collapse himself on his behind and drink with his back to the door. He picked here and there at the Mexican woven welcome mat beneath him.

Walter cupped a cool dry hand round his mouth. "Brenton," he called down. "You feeling alright?"

"Hey." Brenton raised a hand to his brow like a visor though it wasn't bright, "Walter. Didn't see you up there."

"Nope. But here I am anyway. How's it?"

"Alright. Alright. How's Mrs. Lee?"

"She's good."

"Saw that big old bag of yarn you brought in the other day. That to keep the wife out of mischief?"

Walter cupped a hand to his ear. "Say?"

"The yarn. That keep her out of mischief."

"Damn, son. That is her mischief." Walter leaned the broomhandle against the railing and leaned a forearm down to it. He kept the other arm twisted back behind him to knuckle his back. "How's that girl you been having around?"

"Mary. She good."

"She'd be even better I bet if you had her somewhere you could at least look at her."

"Huh? Oh. She don't come round the pad when I drink."

"Well?" Walter asked.

"Well I'm drinking tonight."

"I see. Well she's real nice. Kayla and I like her. Kayla even came outside to say hi and you know the only thing that gets her out the house is gossip. Anyway, Brenton, you look tired. Drunk as a skunk too, but that tired drunk. You quit working so hard."

"Yessir." Brenton raised the bottle to his open mouth and it clinked his teeth. He pulled the bottle back, looked at it like he wanted to slap it right then and there.

"You paid up through to winter here," Walter said. "Why don't I give you some back so you could take a vacation? Bring back one of those mats you're setting on for Kayla. She likes it. For a mat mostly, but maybe to sit on too. Who knows the possibilities?"

"No sir. I'm my own boss. Can't take no vacations."

"Alright then. Heading inside now."

Walter unleaned himself from the railing, or tried too, but ended up using the broomhandle like a cane.

"Why don't you take a vacation, Walter Mr. Lee?"

Walter smiled, twisting his hands round the broomhandle, a coarse sound.

"Oh I don't know. I'm sure I got a long vacation coming just a piece up the highway."

Brenton laughed, a bark really, and shook his head. Janine yelled for them to cut it out out there.

"Where you gonna go?" Brenton asked. "Hawaii or something?"

"Good evening, Brenton." Walter went inside, left Brenton there smiling big.

Brenton kept on drinking. He took a drink and whispered *vacation*, still smiling. Then the smile slipped into something more crooked, and his brow collapsed into its center and he nodded slow.

"Oh. I get it." He tugged himself up by the door's knob. "I get it."

SIXTEEN

June and Kiddy ran along the top of the brick wall that divided the neighborhood backyards from the drive-in parking lot. In one yard a family was grilling. The next had an empty swingset creaking. They passed with their arms out like tightrope walkers.

June called back, "Speed it up past this one." He wondered if the old man still spent nights scaring people off the wall with that shotgun. He remembered him as old even ten years ago, but orneriness and a bitter relationship with the world seemed to him the recipe for a long life.

She had her heelstraps fingerwrapped, toes clapping in her right hand. "I can't go any faster than I'm already going."

The old man's yard was overgrown by fruit trees. An orange near the wall, thorny lemon in the center, a vast dark avocado near the back porch of the house. It was already night on that covered porch though the cooling air they rushed through atop the wall was only grey with dusk. She slowed to admire the view of the sunset over the Mexican tiled rooftops sprawling westward, like some scaled animal stretched out for the last of the sun. Behind them the movie-screen was pink and all of the cars milling about were pink too. Seagulls milled as well, only higher, around the dumpster behind the squat snackshack, or turned higher still, unsure of settling, unsure of this place twenty minutes and a world apart from the coast towns.

"Kiddy," June said. "Hurry up."

When she pivoted it was dancelike and as rigid, and June was coming back for her, struggling to keep his balance while somehow at a dead run. He was pointing down into the yard beneath her where an old man had taken form out of the dark in the porch, might as well have shrugged it from his shoulders like an afghan to reveal a skeletal nose, a ropeveined forearm, the long dark muzzle of a shotgun. He had the butt of the stock pressed to his hip like the lance of a color bearer.

The old man raised the shotgun and settled the stock into his shoulder.

He shouted, "I told you a million times now. Think I don't recognize you? Huh? Think I don't?"

He fired a shot upwards. It seemed almost to fell the night which had crept over the neighborhood and the parking lot in secret. And that was all the shots it took for Kiddy to run down the length of the wall at June who'd been coming to her rescue, so fast he had to turn and run from her to keep from tumbling backwards into the orange tree, being pushed more likely.

She took his hand and hopped down, seemingly unaware that he bore her weight with a hand beneath her arm, as if this was the grace with which she fell under any circumstances.

She slapped his chest. "You could have warned me."

She giggled in a manner that freed her face to look as he hadn't seen it in ten years; not just young, but happy. He smiled.

"What?" she asked.

"I did warn you."

"Did not."

"I said 'watch out.' From now on you know 'watch out' means watch out."

"Watch out," she said.

"Yeah. Like 'here it comes.'"

He lay the blanket out beneath some trees and sat down crosslegged and she did the same beside him. He took the flask from the pocket of his flannel and offered it up.

She undid the cap and drank. Watched the movie. Drank again.

When she handed it back she was moving her lips and he held up a hand to shush her for the time being but lowered the hand instead. On the big screen glowing above the cars black as waterbugs, Rita Hayworth sat playing a guitar and singing. He took the flask from Kiddy and watched as Kiddy mouthed the words, silently at first, but volume rising more and more.

He'd have thought this was a show meant to wrap him around her finger if she didn't seem so suddenly familiar to him. Here she was, the girl he'd left behind that loved singing and music, his music, right here all along. And she was not like her mother had been, a slave to married men's money. And she was not like Rosalina had been, but he couldn't even name that, didn't know what to call that spell.

But maybe the worst of Kiddy didn't come from what those women had been. Maybe the worst was, like him, Kiddy had learned that pretending nothing matters makes you seem indestructible. But that was only the first junction to a road that swallowed headlights like the swirling stuff of souls. He'd already learned where to find the next junction, the next crossroads. Seeming like you don't care only takes you one of two ways. You either stop caring for reals—but no one could do that, could they?—or you go on living at a distance from everyone, a distance beyond miles, ten years gone and still going on.

Kiddy was singing along quietly and his thoughts died, fell to the back of his throat as if her voice had lulled them.

She was singing, "When Mrs. Oleary's car kicked the lantern, in Chicago town, they say that started the fire, that burned Chicago down. That's the story that went around, but here's the real low down."

June interrupted, "Mame kissed a fire from out of town, that kiss burned Clearwater down." She snapped her head to him. "What's that supposed to mean?"

"Faker. A real, real good actress. No doubt. I knew you couldn't go your whole life not liking nothing. I mean, I knew you had to like something. Don't listen to music. Want to be in movies, but don't care which ones."

She didn't speak and he watched her, waiting. Each moment that passed seemed to speed the slide of her eyes from car to car out there, and he thought she might be imagining herself in each, a different shadow among shadows, the different women she could be. He was imagining.

She turned on him then. "What about you? You left as one person and came back another. Who are you supposed to be? You don't seem to like nothing or nobody and what I hear around is nobody likes you."

On the movie screen Gilda had quit singing. You could see the speakerposts at each spot, the wires running from them to the cars' antennas, and the dialogue was staggered by the speakers in the lot as if all carloads of folks spoke in chorus.

"I still like music," he said.

"You ain't played or written one song since you got back, I betcha. Been too busy trying to sing your way into my panties. That's worse than not trying at all, Junie. Trying too hard."

"I've been waiting on a muse, a live thing. You're so cold I got to touch you not for fun, but to make sure you got a pulse. Make sure Brenton shouldn't come out and get you."

"Bout the only reason you would call an old friend, too. Ain't it? Cause June needs something? How the hell you expect me to act? Huh?" She snatched the flask back from him, took a swig, and wiped her mouth with her forearm like a man. "Junie I'm so glad you're back? Junie can I hear your tape? Junie I been waiting. I been waiting just for you. I waited ten years, and I was gonna wait ten more, since that night I said you could have me and you just said no thanks. No thanks don't want it. Well what? You want it now? Stand in line."

"Shut your mouth Kiddy. I ain't standing in no lines."

"I do what I want with my mouth," she said, but she hardly moved anything but her lips.

He grabbed her wrist and she raised the other hand to slap him but he grabbed that wrist too.

"Kiddy," he said. His lips were nearly on hers when he said it: "Watch out."

Brenton said:

Me and Mary were parked at the back of the Drive-In parking lot cause we didn't want the Ferry blocking other peoples' view of the screen. We had the windows rolled down and could feel a cool wind even though that meant we could hear all the other speakers blaring the movie, but rolled up wouldn't work neither cause I had put on too much cologne to stand it. Maybe it wasn't even that it was too much, but that it smelled awful, like a cigar soaked in rubbing alcohol. Cause I had bought it out of some dude's trunk at the Circle K on Flower and Lakewood. He said it was just like Armani but cheaper. Turned out all that shit was was cheaper.

Mary wouldn't quit laughing at me, this big high-pitched laugh that rocked the Ferry. Her hoopearrings jingled and jangled like Christmas.

"Quit laughing," I said, "You messing up my shocks."

She leaned outside the window, pinching her nose and panting like a dog, then started laughing again. The dude in the RV next to us mad dogged her and rolled up his window.

I had a few napkins from the Snack Shack and a Big Gulp cup of Sprite sitting in the cup holders of the center console. I dipped the napkins in Sprite and started scrubbing my neck. "Watch this. This'll do it."

I saw her eyeballing that buttered popcorn in the striped bag on the dash, all steaming up the glass.

"Go on," I said, "get some."

She made a sour face, with her lips pursed and her eyes shut tight. It was like she had to shut her eyes at the popcorn just to have the strength to say, "No. I don't want none."

She crossed her left leg away from me, over the other one. They say that's a real bad sign in the men's magazines.

She was staring at Rita Hayworth on the screen when she said, "I can't. I'm on a diet."

"What diet? For what?"

"It's a no-carb diet."

"Like what you mean? Only meat?"

"Yeah. You could eat whatever you want so long as it ain't got no breads or pastas."

"Shit," I said. "I been on that diet all my life. Carne asada. Steak. Chorizo—"

"—You eat it with tortillas?" she asked.

"—Eggs. What? Hell yeah."

She shook her head. "No tortillas. That's carbs."

I said, "What? It ain't bread!"

She just shook her head again and said it real solemn like, "No tortillas."

I turned down the volume on the radio and Hayworth was a mute cause I couldn't believe this girl was living off eggs and bacon and shit and couldn't eat a goddam piece a toast. I said, "Well then fuck that shit, no tortillas. Why you on a diet anyway? Your stomach is flat."

She smacked her big maroon-painted lips at me. They were shiny. "Don't worry about it, Brenton. Don't you know this is rude conversation?"

"There's no such thing as rude conversation. There's rude people and there's conversations."

"It's none of your business," she said. Her face looked hot. The dark around her eyes wasn't just eyeshadow no more.

"You gossip on the phone all damn day," I said, "and now you don't want to say nothing?"

"It's cause of my ass, okay?" She said it loud and stared out the windshield at the screen. "In case you haven't noticed, I've got a big ass."

The steamed part of the windshield was crawling back down toward the bag of popcorn on the dash. I went back to scrubbing my neck with the Sprite-soaked napkin. I didn't know what to say at first. There was no denying her ass.

"I think this is working," I said. "Now I smell like lemonlime."

"Lemonlime ain't a fruit, Brenton. It's either lemon or it's lime."

"What's wrong with you?" I asked.

She didn't say nothing.

"What's wrong?" I asked again.

"You don't ask girls about that stuff, okay? It's embarrassing."

Her eyes looked shiny like she was gonna cry.

"You know what?" I said. I said, "You do got a big ass. You got a big, fine, round, rotund even, just the right size kind of big ass, baby, and what is wrong with that? You tell me. I don't know. That diet's for valley girls who don't want nothing but skin and bone. You wanna look like the Cryptkeeper? Huh? You wanna look like Skeletor? No way."

"Don't be stupid."

"You don't like what you see in the mirror, maybe you ain't looking at it right. The meat is for the man, baby. The bone is for the dog."

She was laughing now.

I said, "Believe that."

But I could see a tear or two that she had been holding back start to fall down her near cheek, and I tossed my lemonlime napkin away and leaned in to kiss her. She was on me, kissing my lips, my ears, breath all down my neck.

She stopped. "You smell like lemons," she said.

I said, "Lemonlimes. Hey, I got a gurney in the back I keep just for when I need to sleep off hard nights."

She damn near dragged me back there, but just then there was a loud blast somewhere, reminded me of that old man in the neighborhood that chased the ticketskippers off his wall.

"What was that?" she asked. Her hair had fallen down over one side of her face. The other side was smiling big enough for both.

I said it wasn't nothing. She asked if it was a gunshot.

"If we ain't hit then let's get back there," I said. "If we are then let's get back there anyways. Maybe save whoever ferries us the trouble."

Walter said:

We sat our easy chairs side by side, only the end table with that lamp on top between us, Kayla knitting, a story playing on the stereo, and me just scratching my chin.

"It's a Saturday night," I told her.

She didn't say anything.

"You don't want to do nothing?" I asked.

"Mmhmm," she said.

I leaned forward. "Like what?"

She said, "Knit and listen to my story."

I went back to scratching my chin. "Hunh."

After a while she set all her knitting aside, leaned over and stopped the story. In her lap she had a nice sock going now, I could see that. I watched her get up and go round the counter to the fridge. The beers inside the door clinked when she opened it, clinked when she closed it.

She had two beers in each hand and she handed me two, set the other two on the end table. She pressed play on the CD player. That's where she always kept her young Rod Stewart, not the flashy animal print and leather pants stuff, but the early rock. From when he was with Faces. The music started. She turned the dial up.

She took up one of her beers and came over and sat real gentle in my lap. "That hurt your back?"

"Nope."

We both sipped from our beers.

"We don't have to go out to have fun," she said.

This was her game. I said, "Nowhere but the bedroom."

With one hand she cradled the side of my face, a thumb over my ear, the other fingers wrapped round back of my neck.

"Watch you don't throw out your back," she said.

I said, "Watch I don't throw out yours."

The night was cool and dark, and the boxers' skin was flat as matte paint. Spanky bounced on the balls of his feet in the pit. His shoulders swayed like an R&B dancer.

The man facing him could hardly keep his arms at chest level, let alone protect his puffy face. His mustache worked to collect the sweat and the snot from his nose and send it in runnels down either side of his mouth, and he looked like a sad clown.Augustine leaned against the plywood barrier around the pit, wearing a trashbag like a poncho. "I'm here to talk business, Spanky. Come on. You whooped him already."

When Spanky looked at Augustine the man in the pit hooked Spanky with a right. Spit and sweat splattered Augustine's trashbag. Augustine's nostrils flared. His mouth was gaping wide and he looked insulted. He shouted, "Oh that's it. Knock that bitch out."

In the pit, Spanky landed a flurry of blows and the man looked asleep before he even began to fall. When he fell he crumpled in on himself and lay tangled on the dirt floor.

"I hate when they do that," Spanky said. "It doesn't make a sound, you know?"

"Sounded like it hurt."

"But it doesn't make that thump. I like that thump."

"Well you lucky I thought to wear this poncho. If not, you'd have gotten slobber on my new shirt. I'd show you the thump. This shit," he plucked up what would have been the collars of the trashbag if it had had them, "under here, is Gucci. Cost me seventy dollars. You got seventy dollars?"

"I got a lot more than seventy bones." Spanky was tugging a glove off with a bite to the knuckle. "And we'll have more soon."

"You gots to do that with your teeth?" Augustine said. "It's disgusting."

Spanky chucked the red glove at Augustine's belly and he fumbled it. "You gots to wear Gucci around the house?"

* * *

June and Kiddy finished the rest of the movie in silence, huddled together with the blanket over their shoulders. Now and then Kiddy tapped her toe against the top of his boot, but when he looked at her she was staring out at the screen, her eyes flickering with it and lost in the story. Hundreds of cars were spread out before them, people sitting on car roofs, on hoods, in the beds of pickups. The place looked like a refuge.

When the movie was over June folded up the blanket, handed over the flask, and waited. "It's kind of chilly."

She took a drink and screwed the cap down and handed it back. "Not anymore."

She was smiling. He thought she seemed warmed by him, maybe just by the whiskey, but he couldn't be sure.

"I haven't told anyone yet," she said, "but I got a part. An extra, but a part."

June hooked a thumb into a beltloop in his jeans. "In a real movie this time?"

She stuck her face forward. "Yeah." She turned away and raked some hair back over her shoulders. "Sorta. Some mystery horror flick. Supposed to be a comedy too, I don't know."

"It sounds good." He took her wrist and pulled her around to face him. "We should celebrate."

She took his hand off of her but didn't hold it long before she let it drop. "Another date in the bushes or somewhere nice?"

"I got just enough money to keep me out here." He picked at a loose stitch in his boot. "Sooner I spend, sooner I'm gone."

The cars lined up at the exit were honking. The shapes of kids like monkeys hung and swung on the jungle gym beneath the screen. He seemed to be seeing everything but her.

She stood in front of him, her face a patchwork of light and shadow. She said, "I didn't mean it like that. Swear to god."

He led her to the wall and set the blanket over the top for her. "I'll give you a boost."

"Oh no. I ain't gonna pass that old man again. Nice hair don't make a head look good if that head's been blown off a body."

"He ain't out once the movie's done. Kind of a drunk. Just passes out on that porch."

"How do you know all that?"

"Brenton and I used to come out here every night when we were at Clearwater Junior High. One summer, we were like fourteen, it was every single night."

She stepped on his forward leaning thigh and pushed herself up to stand on the wall.

He went on: "Old man wasn't there every night, just most. Word was every now and then cops would take him in for shooting, but you know how it is here. You could shoot all night and the cops wouldn't come less you were shooting at them. Me and Brenton would dare each other who could stand on that old man's piece of wall the longest before we got scared or shot at or both. Usually both."

When she'd stepped aside and took up the blanket he pulled himself up too. He stood wiping his hands on the back of his jeans.

"Brenton always won. He couldn't stand to lose to me so it was best that way anyway. Once he lasted thirteen seconds and two warning shots. I think his trick was he shut his eyes. I couldn't never do that."

"You all are stupid."

"Oh, the old man wouldn't kill no one. He fires straight up. Maybe kill a seagull by accident, that's it."

They walked more slowly this time, her leading. She spoke to one shoulder, "You know a lot about this random old man."

"Longer you live, longer word's been getting around about you. Heard he lived there before they even built the drive-in."

"He's old."

"Old as dirt, I bet. Older. Say the house got broken into back in ninety-four, some Eastsiders broke in and they smashed all the pictures of his old lady, she was dead by then, say they stole all her jewelry he'd been keeping and that sort of kicked something loose in his head."

She smacked her lips. "That's messed up."

"Yeah, but who knows with these things, right? Urban myths."

She stopped, turned around to face him. "You think it's true?" They both stood like statuary in the glossy glow from the screen. Below them the old man's yard seemed a dark pool, a swamp out of which trees grew to catch breath.

He said, "What? That he's been waiting for one night, when he'll vengeance his true love?"

She smiled and shrugged her shoulders clear up to her ears. "It's romantic, right?"

"Romantic maybe, but true? Hell no. That old movie we watched wasn't even as sappy as all that."

"I thought you were a romantic?"

"I am. For you."

"Now who's sappy?"

They both walked along the wall, ghost-circus tight-ropers. She stopped again.

He stutter-stepped against his momentum.

She asked, "Not for no one else?"

Then the blast beneath them tore the yard open like a parting of dark waters. They saw the old man for an instant on the porch, shotgun in hand, heard the buckshot like a hive of bees, and all went black again. They jumped off the wall.

They stood on the asphalt of the parking lot looking at the wall. Above it, the treetops silver wrought in the moonlight. The sound of their panicked breathing.

June smiled where she couldn't see. "Not one, not ever."

SEVENTEEN

Cross-town rivalry wasn't the name for it. Spanky lived no more than a mile from Junie. His was one of the few houses on a street called Bixler, lined with duplexes, triplexes, and fewer still with any yard. If you knew the neighborhood, you knew that it was no surprise that his house was not the only one painted lime green.

The property was closed in by a chainlink fence, and tidy. A dirt run on one side and a driveway on the other took you into a backyard and seemingly another country, where laws and languages and blood commingled, where a horde of men stood round a pit betting on fighting dogs. The men bared their teeth too, as if to bite should the vig begin to drop. Fists, overhanging the plywood wall, clenched dollars.

Against a back wall, still more dogs slept in kennels. Up against the house, there'd been built out of scrapwood and old billboards a ramshackle grandstand, and on the top-most bench of this Spanky perched, elbows on widespread knees, asserting even while seated the space of many men, chewing on a splintered red and white plastic bar straw.

Augustine sat a few steps below him, his legs crossed demurely so that one of his snakeskin boots was at all times aloft and in sight.

Spanky was saying, "Don't worry about my shit, okay? My shit is the bomb."

Augustine smacked his lips. "I'm worried about my cheddar, baby, and that shit you had last month was bammer. Junie didn't need to steal that weed when he stole my pad, okay? I gave him that bammer. I said, *here you go, baby, you moving into my place, might as well have what's in the cupboard.* That shit was so weak I left it up by the coffee. Thought it was some Sleepy-Time Tea. My middle name ain't Celestial Seasonings, nigger. Is yours?"

"I didn't know."

The horde around the pit lowed. A fat man turned away with bright blood splattered across his forehead. In the pit a large black pit bull had another, tiger-striped, pinned—

jaws clenched round the throat, shaking its head as if to tear free, blood seeping from fur as if wrung from a sponge.

"You didn't know what?"

"That it was bad."

"Man, you could have learned that weed was bammer from Anne of Green Gables."

"I don't smoke, man. I don't do nothing. I hardly even drink." Spanky took a bottle of water from a cooler full of beer and let its lid creak shut. "It's poison." Spanky took the gnarled straw from his mouth, drank, and put it back.

"While I admire your puritanical discipline," Augustine said, taking a few snuffs off a pinky nail and replacing the cap on a vial. "Don't it make for a bad business model?"

"Maybe. That's where you come in. Me? I just worry about my dogs. Last week, my baby over there…" Spanky pointed to the garage. Its open door showed its raftered guts where a small boy stood laboratorially by a treadmill. A mercurially coated, malletheaded pitbull ran the treadmill with a weight-vest wrapped round its torso, a single weightplate dangling by a chain beneath its slobbering jaw, "…he won me two matches at five to one, cause he's smaller than most. But he's strong. The vig was at a thousand bones a match. I got three more dogs got me a vig of three fifty, and four more after that, that brought in fifty more."

"How much was that total?"

"A fucking ton. You should start writing this shit down, you know?"

"What am I, your secretary?"

"I been thinking about that. With all that cash I got some speed, I got some coke, I got some bomb Humboldt Chronic. None of that Compton niggerweed."

"Watch your fucking mouth, *homes*." Augustine slid his head from side to side. "Don't you know my daddy's black? Pull that nigger shit I'll scratch that stache off your face. Who you think you is, anyway, Pancho Villa?"

Spanky grinned. He shrugged.

The men around the pit had scattered about the yard to talk and smoke and drink the beer Spanky had a teenaged girl selling from ice chests in the kitchen.

In the pit a man was spraying a fine mist of water from a hose while others tamped the dirt with two by fours.

The bloodied and whimpering dog had been wrapped like butcher's meat in newspaper and set in a wheelbarrow beside the garage.

The boy left the garage and came to stand beside the bleachers, raised a hand to his eyes to block the sun but it looked a salute, and called out to Spanky, "Which ones should I gives to him?"

"Four across, five down."

"Okay."

The boy turned and ran back to the garage, inside of which a faceless limbless mannequin modeled Spanky's apron. The boy counted carefully across and down to find the correct pocket, and removed a vial. He took a syringe from a jar of them resting on a board shelved across two sawhorses. Beside that jar there were others filled with gauze or cotton or rubber tubing.

The boy ran out onto the grass. At the wheelbarrow, he jabbed the needle into the vial, pulled the plunger back, lifted the needle to his eye to watch for the bead, and then jabbed the dog through the newspaper wrapping without any ceremony. As he went back inside the garage, he tossed everything into a trashcan beside the treadmill.

Outside, in the wheelbarrow, the swollen newspaper had ceased its rise and fall.

A worn leather boot bluéd at the heel by a jean-hem, stepped up onto the bottom bench. "Hey, Augustine," June said. He flicked a piece of grass off the boot-toe with a middle-finger. "Hey, Spanky."

Without looking, Augustine smiled in recognition, as if he'd been expecting this, and said, "That's my cheddar."

June looked up from his boot. He shook his head in a way that meant *I like you, but I don't like the things you say and it's your responsibility to change.* What he actually said was, "Find a new place yet?" June was looking at Augustine, thinking maybe he'd been too hard on the guy. He was surprised that Augustine hadn't yet come back to haunt him.

Both Spanky and Augustine looked down at June who'd come to stand before them seemingly from nowhere, and they with the lost look, as if caught in the act—of what, they looked to each other to discern—until their right to be here welled up both their chests.

"Me?" June said. "I'm settling in just fine."

Behind June, the horde had parted to stare at his back, and through the tunnel of men you could see two new dogs fighting their harnesses before the men behind them cut them loose and from opposite sides of the pit the dogs shot like stones from slings to collide with yawps behind and obscured by June, who hadn't once quit leaning on his up-raised knee. Eyes closed, he was listening to the snarls and yelps of the dogfight, consulting that old shitlist or hitlist or whatever he kept in his head.

When June finally looked up, Spanky stood. Spanky glanced once at the dogfight, spat, looked at June.

"June. June bug. Junie. I hope you ain't here to apologize about my whore. That was a long, long time ago. She knew she was too big for the second story. She told me so. I didn't listen. But you got to know she was and that it wasn't your fault. You got to know a lot. You got to have a lot. You got to have balls to come here uninvited. Must have a pussy too, cause you're really fucked."

June looked up then, not a motion of the head but a slow upturn of the eyes, and dusted off the toe of his boot with one hand. "How do you keep track of all of them?"

"Huh?" Spanky had one side of his lip curled. He seemed to be sniffing the air for some clue as to what had brought June here after ten years at least. Maybe toss in a few weeks that Spanky might not have known about, June keeping it on the down low that he was trying to get to Kiddy.

June said, "How do you know, say, a winning dog from a losing one?"

Augustine slid his gaze from June's boots to the collar of his red and black flannel. "In this case," Augustine said, "the losing one's got awful style." He giggled and adjusted the fall of his Prince t-shirt. He squeezed the crotch of his toothwhite jeans.

June smiled and turned up the collar of his flannel which it was too hot to be wearing and which he knew set him apart in that yard, hood, and world of baggy cholo clothes or flashy vaquero gear. He looked at Spanky and said, "He ain't talking about me, is he?"

Spanky said, "What do you want, whiteboy?"

The horde around the pit had begun to shift toward the grandstand, as if they sensed a new pit and new dogs to throw in it.

"You know I ain't a whiteboy and I ain't a cholo so don't try to punk me like neither."

Spanky came down the steps and they creaked each one and dust fell beneath his tennis shoes. He jumped down and landed on both feet before June. Their chests were touching. He was staring bug-eyed at June and he smelled of hard-water and locker-room soap. "Well? You got something to say? Maybe start by saying *sorry I sent you to juvie.* Maybe start there. That's where I really learned to punch, bitch. That's where I learned to watch my ass."

"Yeah. That's all I come to do. To say. Stay away from Kiddy. I don't want you seeing her no more."

"I don't see her, man. She sees me."

"Well she ain't looking for you no more. So nobody's seeing nobody."

Spanky laughed, turned to face the crowd, smiled and swiped his hand down his mustache, but when he turned back to June he'd brought his fist with him. June crumpled to the ground with his own hand pressed to his jaw.

Sound stopped. The horde jeered silently. A man with hands on his belly opened his mustached mouth so wide in silent laughter that June could see his silvered molars. Then sound swelled outward from somewhere inside June's head and some men called him names in English. Some in Spanish. Fingers pointed.

Augustine was snickering, adjusting the fall of his pantlegs over his snakeskin boots. "Damn! And you were so pretty, baby."

Spanky was waving a finger in the air. "I was featherweight champ in L.A. County fifteen years ago, and I been waiting to sock you again since the first time." Spanky slammed his fists together with a meaty pop. "That shit felt amazing."

June fought his flickering eyelids so he wouldn't look stunned, but calm, patiently waiting on the time to stand.

"Did you hear the thump?" Spanky called.

Augustine said, "Oh, I heard it, baby."

June had only looked at any one man fleetingly. The realization seemed to settle on Spanky's bald head and burn like the sun that since June had arrived he'd been studying the yard, the pit, the dogs in their kennels, the prized dog being brushed down now by the boy in the shade of the garage.

"Get up," Spanky said. He held his right fist before his face and rocked it back and forth. "Get the fuck out of here."

"Before you what?"

"What do you expect me to say? Before I kill you?" Spanky raised his arms to the crowd around the pit. "Do I look like I'm crazy or something?"

Every man around the pit shook his head *no,* the way they might if asked out of the blue had they ever cheated on their women.

June stood and dusted himself off. Still he looked at no one. He squinted up at a palm tree that had grown side by side with a telephone pole and the tops of both flared in the sun which was like a white hot coin.

Augustine now stood hipslung with a hand in his back pocket and that elbow chickenwinged.

June asked him, "What they do to these dogs to make them so mean?"

Augustine smiled. "You a crazy son of a bitch, Junie." He blew June a kiss and June rolled his eyes. "What do you mean what they do? What else would you do? You kick they ass. From the get go you take it to them."

June turned to go then, smiling—a big smile, a slow turn—and finally eyeballed each and every man in one impossible moment before he headed down the dirt run at the side of the house, rubbing his jaw. Then he was gone altogether, the echo of his words perhaps in each man's ear because they were all silent, seemed still to be listening to him.

That's what I thought you did, June had said. *What happens when it backfires?*

EIGHTEEN

Came days when Spanky was often seen at Walter's apartment complex knocking on doors, and neither June nor
Kiddy went out of them. A week went by. Two. No one
saw the new couple, but everyone knew where they were.
Janine would stand in her doorway wearing her new bank-
teller's outfit, which hid the few lumps of her aging figure
well, and smile at Spanky and say, "I told you, she's suppos-
ably a grown woman. How am I suppose to know where
she stay at, and for who? For what? For nothing." And then
she'd roll her eyes up to June's door, maybe stab the air with
a cigarette.

And Spanky knocked on June's door at night, and in
the morning, and at midday. Behind Spanky's back people
began to make jokes that June and Kiddy were in there,
but couldn't hear his knocking for all the knocking boots

of their own. Two policemen had arrived and stood behind Spanky with their thumbs hooked into their belts and their heads cocked sideward in curiosity. He'd looked at the 40oz bottle of malt liquor in his hands as if it had been handed to him by someone else, and said, "Man, I don't even drink. And this, it tastes like shit." They escorted Spanky down the stairs and off the premises and him shouting threats up to June even as he left.

You could see Kayla watching through the gap in the blinds she'd made with two fingers. She had the phone tucked between her chin and shoulder, was talking to someone, perhaps narrating the events as they passed, and even after it was all done she didn't quit looking.

Sometimes, in the clusters of men gathered round the dogpit, jokes were made at Spanky's expense. Spanky's dogs won often enough that he was considered by most in the barrio to be a rich man. He could afford the best dogs, sell the best drugs, make himself a richer man and, in turn, a bigger target of jokes.

He'd since hired Augustine to follow him around like a secretary, recording everything Spanky said in a spiral-bound memopad with a zebra-print pencil.

He was dictating one day from the top of the grand-stand: Augustine scribbling furiously, Spanky's eyes on the pit. That day a rare cockfight was to serve as the opening entertainment.

The crowd was thin. One ring, around the plywood barrier of the pit. The crowd would be four men deep and constricting like a snake around the pit by the time his prized dog fought.

Two cockwranglers, dark men in worn clothes with soft widebrimmed hats pulled low, stood by the garage with a cage each at their feet. In each cage was a rooster. A thin leather rope tethered a rooster's scabby leg to its cage. One of the cockwranglers knelt in the grass, cooing, untied the tether, and opened the cage-door. He waited until the rooster had ducked around to face away and he reached inside and brought it out onto the grass.

The cockwrangler thumbed a tight grip on the tether.

The rooster's comb and wattle had been sheared off, and now puckered scar tissue ridged the top and bottom of its head. White flesh, hard as a thumbnail, shelled its one blinded eye. Red-orange feathers patched its back like an old moth-eaten coat—wounds patched its back too—its legs and stomach were plucked for fashion, to give sight to the rooster's musculature, and to ease the attachment of the razorspurs replacing the flesh spurs, sheared off with all the other excess.

The rooster looked sleek, forward leaning, chest out, head bobbing side to side. Its feathers were red fading to orange at the head, like the rooster was fire if fire could strut.

The cockwrangler took the rooster up once more and set it on a rusty scale by the wall of the garage. The other cockwrangler did likewise with one of his. It was too heavy. He put it back and got the other. Still too heavy. He wiped his sweating brow, and got another.

There were few present to witness the insult that caused Spanky to sit up, to go pale as a pitdog's spilled gut, to stand, and to descend the grandstand. The men ignored the cockwranglers as they entered the pit, began prepping the cocks by bringing them just outside of bloodletting range. It was the fiery one versus a black one. The black one hopped and backed away like a punch-drunk boxer's ducking head.

Spanky hadn't had to ask who'd uttered the insult, a variation on the tired joke that he'd grown goat horns, an implication that the chupacabra was alive and well and living in the barrio. Right here, in Clearwater. And she's found a new goat to suck.

The men who hadn't made the joke created a sudden and vast space around the one who had, and he couldn't shrink the distance between them no matter which way he stepped. When he finally faced Spanky he smiled a weak smile that raised his broomy mustache the way some men raise eyebrows, as if to say, well, what now?

But Spanky didn't see him. Or pretended not to. If anything, by the time he stood shoulder to shoulder with the man—Spanky staring into the pit and the man still looking back on the grandstand—the color had returned to Spanky's face. The two men might as well have been not only facing different directions, but been inhabiting different places, in a different time.

Spanky wrapped his left arm around one of the few support posts of the pit's plywood barrier. He told the cockwranglers to bring the roosters closer together and, by degrees, they did.

The fiery rooster struck with scalloped yellow feet at the black. The razorspurs fitted to its feet hissed when they cut the shrinking air. They rang when they clashed steel on steel with the black's spurs raised in weak defense. The sound of it made the innermost ear itch. The fiery rooster's wings flapped and clapped against the arms of the man who struggled to hold it, the veins in his forearms rising like ropes gone taut.

Spanky said, "Stop there. That's good." He swiped the sweat from his nose with a knuckle. "Beautiful bird."

He braced his left arm around the post as if he had it in a headlock, and shot a stiff right arm out across the insulting man's chest. The man's eyes popped wide just before Spanky clotheslined him over the barrier. His heels shot skyward. He fell into the pit.

"Make your bets," Spanky said. "If he tries to get out, push him back in. If he tries to kill that red one, kill him first. I want to buy it when it's done with his face."

Spanky had turned and walked away then, a few feathers drifting into the air behind him and above him like confetti fanfare in his wake.

But it was just the man in the pit screaming as Spanky ascended the bleachers, folded himself into a comfortable sitting position from which he might watch.

Augustine sat, legs crossed tightly and the memopad resting on his thigh. He was staring at the zebra-print pencil, spinning it round between his fingers so it looked hypnotizing.

"I think he got what he deserved," Augustine mumbled. He rolled his eyes back and whistled *cuckoo, cuckoo*.

"It's not like I killed him. He'll fight his way out eventually." Spanky seemed to lose himself in the grotesque show below. After a moment he said, "Hey, Augustine?"

Augustine, who'd been taking a bump off the sharp arm of a bic pen-cap, looked up. "Yes, dear?"

"Write down in your little diary how long it takes before he cries for his moms. It's good research."

"Okay. What's moms in Spanish again? Is it mamma?"

"Don't worry, stupid. Just count. And give me some of that, too, while you're at it."

Augustine leaned away from him. "You sure about that?"

"You're not counting." Spanky held out his hand. Augustine reached over with the screw-top vial and the pen-cap, singsonging, *one alligator, two alligators*...and the man in the pit screamed, but no one helped, so the man went right on screaming.

NINETEEN

Spanky's finger pressed the small black button of his neighbor's doorbell. The wooden door was open inside but the steel security door was closed. The dark shape of a fat man lumbered over to stand behind it.

An *I Love Lucy* rerun blared from the TV in the living room. A small Pomeranian scrabbled over the linoleum in the entryway. It barked once, twice. In the background, Lucy had some 'splaining to do.

The dark shape scratched its belly and said, "Spanky."

"Whatsup, neighbor."

"Whatsup?" He craned his neck to look over Spanky's shoulder.

Augustine was standing in the courtyard of the triplex. His fitted t-shirt didn't quite reach his jeans' low waistline and there was a line of tightly coiled hair showing on his belly. He was scribbling in the memopad and every now and then put the zebra-print pencil to his bottom lip, looked up and to the left for an answer. When it came to him he'd tap the pencil to his temple and resume scribbling.

"Who's the mamón?" the neighbor asked Spanky.

"Him?" Spanky swiped his red nose, lipsmacked and said, "That's just my secretary. So I'm here to let you know, if you haven't been noticing, we're having lots of parties at the pad. Lots of noise, you know?"

"Noises?" the dark shape asked. He kicked a slippered foot at the Pomeranian. It scurried away, barked from a safe distance.

"Yeah." Spanky shrugged. He pulled his face into itself and nodded from side to side. He showed his palms and laughed. "You know. Noises."

Spanky reached deep into his sagging pocket and pulled out a wad of bills. He held them tenderly in his palm like a mossy stone he was about to skip.

The steel security door opened, and a belly lead a long procession of flesh onto the porch. The neighbor stood in a baggy blue Dodgers shirt that hung down over his boxer shorts. "Noises. Like music, and chicas, and party noises?"

"Yeah." Spanky pressed the thick wad of bills into the man's fat hand. He sniffed. He bobbed his head like even now he were in a fight with someone. "Tell the rest of the neighbors. Noises like that."

TWENTY

June and Kiddy were naked on the plush couch. The sheet hung up for a curtain filtered the moonlight into a mist, softened their edges like a closeup in an old film. Her dark hair fell over his chest into an inkpool beneath his upraised arm. He was trying to light the cigarette he thrust out with pursed lips at the lighter that would only spark, draw the bones of his face out of the misty light for a flash.

"Don't you know that's how most fires start, in bed?"

He'd had the bed thrown out and he'd moved the monstrous red thing into the bedroom for something to sleep on. It was big enough for two and room to spare.

"I watched for fires all summer." He crossed his eyes down his nose. "I'll watch this one close."

She smiled. "Yeah? What did you do with them? Put them out?"

"Oh no." He smoked. "Not me."

"I know. You do, what's that they always do in Angeles National, control burns?"

"That's what they call it." He finally got the cigarette lit and he set the plastic lighter on the end table. "But really you're just letting it burn. You just coax it to burn in the right direction."

He thought through it again. Her straddling the arm of the couch and him behind, his arm wrapped around front to touch her. Her rocking above him and his hands cradling her. Then him on top of her, grinding out her moans and his. June had called Kiddy his, and she'd slapped him playfully. They'd both gasped into coming soon after.

The sheet had begun to rise between his legs.

He took another drag, blew smoke up and watched it turn in the lamplight. "It's not cigarettes, it's lightning, then arson second, at least out in the forest. It's nature and men burn things up. Which do you think does it more and which does it on purpose?"

"Why don't you quit smoking?" she said. "It's bad for you."

"You're bad for me. I haven't quit playing with you."

She sat up, tugged the sheet up and around her breasts, clutching it at her throat. Her nipples showed faint pink either side of her forearm. "I ain't bad for you. And this ain't playing." She traced a line down the curve of his back. "Is it?"

"You sure?"

She nodded.

"Okay." He took a long drag and held his breath and put the cigarette out on an empty half a pint of whiskey on the floor. Some ash had dusted the couch cushion and he brushed it away. The empty bottle made the room smell like oak, like spice, and a little like bile. Next to the bottle, there was a full pack of cigarettes. Scattered around, his clothes and hers. When he said, "I quit," the smoke seeped out and the room seemed the setting of some foggy dream where men and women could quit bad habits that easy.

"Really?" she asked.

"Sure thing. You want it, you got it." He smiled; that had probably been true of Kiddy as soon as she'd learned that hips could sway. He was nodding, agreeing with his own thoughts. "You know, you're different than your moms. I knew it as soon as I got back, but I couldn't pin it down. Couldn't be sure. You got more. . ."

"Don't talk about my mom, Junie. Don't say shit about her."

"You got more something."

"She works at a bank now, okay? It doesn't make her a good person but it makes her a normal one."

"I'm not dogging on her. I'm complimenting you."

"By saying I'm better?"

"I didn't say better. I said different." He knew now how it sounded. That he wanted, perhaps more than believed, that it was true. "Look, all I said was something about you is different."

She slid back down onto her side, still clutching the sheet in one hand and with the other hand thrumming her fingers on his chest. She was beautiful always but especially when vexed and her brow sank and her lips pursed and she made a small sound in her throat like a moan.

He lifted his head off the arm of the couch, "What?"

"I didn't want to tell you, and now I really don't. I need to go to Spanky's."

He propped himself up on both elbows. "No you don't." He started groping around on the floor, found the cigarette butt he'd rubbed out, and put it on his lower lip. He took up the lighter.

She was on her knees now, and her hands were gesturing under the sheets. "My shoot's day after tomorrow. All my best clothes are there. Augustine helped me pick out my wardrobe special. All my makeup's there. My fucking kiboodle's there, Junie."

"Oh no." He scraped his thumb against the lighter but it only sparked. "Not the kiboodle."

"Yeah. I won't even talk to him, swear to God."

"No."

She leaned over and the sheet fell away. Her breasts swayed a little when she plucked the cigarette from his mouth. "What do you mean, *no?* I'm being nice about this. I could go anyways."

"But you won't." He sat up and took his jeans off the floor and stood into them. He took the bottle up and tilted it to see if anything collected in the corner but nothing did so he tossed it away. He took the cigarettes up, kept the pack and the lighter palmed and took them with him to the bathroom, turned the light on and ran the water in the sink. He shuffled things around and shook a cigarette up out of the pack.

He watched himself smoke while he lathered up a bar of soap. Ran a razor over his soapy face a few times, left the razor in the sink, and slid the mirrored door of the cabinet aside to stash the lighter and the pack. When he slid the door closed again he saw in the mirror that she was standing right behind him, no sheet at all.

With the cigarette balanced on a first knuckle, June pointed a finger at Kiddy's reflection. "You ain't going over there, understand?"

She pressed a foot against the inside of the other knee. "Technically, you weren't pointing at me."

"Well, watch out one of you don't make the other an accomplice in anything dirty."

"You coming back to bed?" she asked. "I mean, the couch. It's late."

He blew smoke into their reflections.

"I can't believe you kept Augustine's couch. He loved that couch. He'd be pissed you moved it."

"I'm not keeping it hostage. He could come get it. I let you take him that tacky seventies lamp he had hanging in the living room."

"He ain't worried about it right now. Spanky's making him all kinds of money." She'd taken a breath to go on, but let it go, as if she'd decided to change the direction of this conversation and needed new breath with which to do it. "Why do you shave in the night and the morning?"

"I'm not sure."

"You always smoke when you do it?"

"No."

"Well, I thought you were quitting," she said.

"I thought so too." He plucked the cigarette off his bottom lip and flicked it in the toilet to hiss. "It appears to me that some things start back up when you ain't looking."

TWENTY-ONE

Walter said:

I wasn't doing work cause like I told Kayla my back wasn't doing too good. I don't quite know what to do most of the time. Kayla's got her knitting and her stories. If I occupy myself by complaining to her she says, *Go to the doctor.*

Said that this morning, *Go to the doctor, Walter, get yourself some of that grass.* I said *Doctors prescribe marijuana cigarettes now?* She said *mmhm. United Republic of California. First to legalize medicinal cannabis.* She said it helps with joint pain. Said it helps even for cancer. I told her I don't know about all that. She said, *least if you were smoking you'd be doing something.* I said *if I did smoke and my back did get better we'd be doing something else. Dirty till dead,* I said. She said, *Be sure and shut the door all the way, there's a draft.*

So the first thing out the door I saw that friend of Kiddy's, Daisy, sitting on the diving board with a pair of scissors in her hand and reading a magazine. One of those glossy girls' magazines. I headed down the steps to tell her this isn't a barbershop, the barbershop's by the bar where it should be.

"You don't live here, right?" I asked.

"Nope."

"Well what're you doing here?"

"Waiting on Kiddy."

"So you two can cut your hairs and let them fill up that pool?"

She squinted up at me with the magazine at her forehead like a visor. "Uh huh."

"Un uh. I got to clean all that out now. I ought to make you do it. I could have my wife knit a blanket out that hair for every welfare baby in this town and still have leftovers. Get off of there now."

But she didn't move because a door slammed overhead and she looked up. I tried to, but I had to turn my whole body around, and by that time whoever it'd been was stomping down that stairwell toward us like his shoesoles were caked over, which is to say like he was in deep shit. I was not surprised when Junie came on toward us.

"Either of you see Kiddy around?"

158

Daisy said, "I been waiting on her ass all afternoon. Thought she was with you last night."

Junie just told her last night was last night.

She said, "We supposed to be cutting our hair."

I said to her, "No you're not. You're not supposed to be cutting anything but loose of my building. Get off that diving board now, it's old and it's dangerous."

She said, "That makes two of you."

Junie gnawed on his bottom lip and he went on past us without saying *excuse me* and that ain't like him and he went to Janine's door, but before he could knock with the tight fist he was wielding Daisy said, "She ain't there. And I called her moms at the bank and she don't know where she is neither. Said she took off early this morning. Had to pick up some clothes or something. I think she said her kiboodle."

I told the girl to come on and I put my hand out and she took it. I groaned. She looked lighter than she was, like how a sow can look cuddly. "What's a kiboodle?"

Junie came back across the courtyard to us. "It's a thing for—I think you keep stuff in it. Lady stuff."

I was staring down into that pool. Beneath the diving board there was a whole carpet of those girls' hair. Months worth. I couldn't even get down in there, let alone be able to clean it out. I wasn't gonna pay no one neither. I ain't loaded. And Junie was always so polite so I said, "Junie, could I ask you a favor?"

"Anytime but now, Walter. You want to catch up with me tomorrow? Right now I got a situation on my hands."

"I know all about that. It's my hands I want to discuss. And my back."

"Tomorrow, Walter. I promise."

He ran out the courtyard and we watched him go.

"I don't know what her problem is." Daisy wrapped the scissors in the magazine and stuffed it all into the back pocket of her jeans. It took a while. Looked like a tight fit.

"What problem?" I asked. "Who's?"

"Kiddy. She's really asking for it and I don't wanna tell her I told her so but I told her. Ever since she been seeing him." She glared at the front door still swinging shut as if Junie stood there still.

I said, "Young woman, why's it take you a pocketful of words to make a penny's worth of sense?"

"I'm saying. She's asking for it."

"She sure is," I said. I started to take a liking to Daisy, just then.

And she said, "Every week she goes without this cut, her hair grows point twelve inches. You know what that's gonna do to her future? It's already been three weeks!"

Daisy huffed off with that rolled magazine in her pocket smacking her back with each step. I just stood out there staring at the wind-rowed hair in the bottom, looking a little like the forest floor, looking like the shapes of things in there. Grass. Wilderness. Until Kayla called me up to order us in some dinner. I always found it's easier to leave a job undone if you get called from it. Otherwise you're just quitting.

TWENTY-TWO

Spanky's backyard was crowded so June had slipped in unnoticed, but before June could land the second punch on Spanky's face Spanky danced away shaking out his arms, and the other men descended upon June. They only had him about the arms at first. Then one had him from behind in a bearhug that was already crushing his ribs. He saw spots in the air that he imagined looked just like the holes ribtips punched through lung tissue.

June caught Augustine's shin with a boot toe and Augustine yelped and brought his hand to his mouth. June hadn't come to hurt Augustine, but the man had scrambled into his way sometime after the bearhug, and June wanted out. Had things not unraveled into chaos so fast he might even have apologized. Then they had him by the legs too. Had him suspended and tugged in all directions.

He spat his words through clenched teeth: "Where is she?"

Spanky had gone up to sit at the top of the grandstand. He wore his apron over a bare chest and a pair of shiny boxing trunks. Tattoos scaling most of his body. The Loc sunglasses were too dark to see into. He lifted a hand to touch his reddening jaw but saw June looking at him, and lowered the hand and shifted his jaw from side to side instead. "Who?"

"You know."

"Everything here's mine. Right now you're mine. If there's something that was yours here, it's not yours anymore, *me entiendes?*"

"Fuck you."

"I don't want him."

The men surrounding June were all of a piece. They were ten feet, some in Jordans, some in Kemps, some in ostrich leather, they were silk blouses and cotton t-shirts and Raiders caps or cowboy hats, and they were gripping his arms, the collar of his flannel, his thighs, his ankles and his boots. They surged outward, each one heading to the street by a different course and June cursed and thrashed in their arms.

He saw the cement pass beneath him. A cluster of basketball shoes and cowboy boots stepped him out over the driveway. He could tell by a brief view of front lawn that he should clench his jaw and brace himself for a tumble on the asphalt, maybe a speedbump in the face. Right on down the slope of the driveway, he went. Then the black asphalt unrolled beneath him. Down that panoramic street chrome-wheeled cars stretched wide, and telephone poles leaned, squat, beneath that immense sky—all thanks to his dog's eye view.

Everyone stopped moving, and he swayed, suspended by weakening grips and limblocks. A pair of highheeled snakeskin boots stepped into sight. Someone tugged June's head back and he saw tight white jeans, a large beltbuckle in the shape of a rose. A small soft hand touched June's jaw and raised his head until he was staring at Augustine's face—the sharply trimmed mustache, the jawline beard.

Augustine whispered, "I know you punked me, and I ain't killed you yet cause Kiddy's been with Spanky a long time and in that time she's told me all about you. She'd never take me shopping anymore if I killed you. When you fools buy her shit that don't fit who you think she give it to? She listened to me when men didn't treat me right. She's too good for this neighborhood and even you got to know that. But until she take off from here, which one day she will, I've got to tell you to stay away."

June shook his head and tried again to break free but Augustine clawed June's head back by the jaw and slapped June three times, the last one the hardest, loud, as if his hand exploded onto June's cheek. He told the men to drop June and they lifted him a bit, then tugged him down and let go just to give the fall momentum. June felt a brief wind and the sound of impact was deep and resonant in his head even as he groaned and tried to suck in air through a gaping mouth he could not stretch wide enough.

Augustine said, "Junie, listen to me, okay? Spanky fed a man to the chickens the other day. I didn't know chickens could do the things they did. I ain't never going to be the same after that shit. That chicken dude ain't never going to be the same, neither. Those chickens fucked him up."

June coughed and that was what finally broke whatever barrier there had been between the air outside of his body and the vacuum within. He sucked in and coughed and sucked again. He rose onto his knees and elbows, ropes of spit like reins hanging from his mouth.

"You too stubborn," Augustine said. "No reason in you. You want what you want just like Spanky." Augustine smacked his lips and put a hand on his hip and pointed down at June from in front of the setting sun. June was squinting up at Augustine, eyes unfocused, trying to discern was Augustine the source of all the red light crawling over the street. Augustine wagged his finger. "You the reason I went back to snatch, Junie. Men like you and Spanky. You all make a fag see something special about pussy."

Augustine's heels clicked over the asphalt and away.

TWENTY-THREE

That night, June sat in the Ghia a block down from Spanky's, with the opened flask between his legs and Art Laboe's oldies-show quiet on the radio. Al Green's "Jesus Is Waiting" had hit its crescendo, and June eased a bit, willing to wait for as long as this song took. But then the old man Laboe himself interrupted the song to make radio time and announce the next dedication.

Most of the duplex and triplex buildings still had a few glowing windows. The nearest house had the front door open but the steel security door shut, and you could see the light inside as if through lace. A small dog's paws skittered across linoleum. An old rerun of I Love Lucy almost drowned out the Ghia's radio.

These oldies were short songs. It would be a new one soon.

June took a drink from the flask and tucked it back between his legs. The stuff was so awful he wasn't sure it wasn't predrunk whiskey rebottled, bile and all. A belch rumbled up from his anxious gut and the drink burned all over again like a match lit in his nose. He'd been buying cheaper and cheaper drink to make his money last, to prolong his time in Clearwater, to make these last few weeks work with Kiddy. He could chart his progress or decline in that matter, by distillery. Makers. Jack. Jim. On down to Kessler, at nearly half the price of the first. From Black Velvet down was a sudden and hard drop, and he was heading down, down, down. There weren't many things he could give Kiddy, maybe none but this. Bust her free and see if she could make it out in Hollywood.

Spanky shut himself inside the bedroom with Kiddy and locked the door with the hand that wasn't weighed down by the forty ounce bottle of Old English malt liquor. There was a chainlock up high and he locked that too. There was a bolt that was meant to run into the floor. He stepped on that and it slid in coldly.

He said, shaking his head, "Got to be careful in this day and age. There's motherfucking criminals every motherfucking where."

He turned to face Kiddy where she lay on the bed. He drank from the bottle of Old E, swiped his mouth with his forearm, and staggered to the foot of the bed. He stood on the balls of his feet as usual, and he ducked his head side to side now, as if avoiding punches only he could see. Maybe just ducking her looks.

She wore a classy shirt with a collar and a pair of nice highheels but all she wore between those were yellow cotton panties. She'd been trying on outfits all day for tomorrow's shoot, though Spanky had told her that he'd never let her go. Clothes lay in disarray about the room.

There were shoes in a small pile at Spanky's feet and he kicked them out of the way. "I like that outfit best."

She didn't look at him. She stared instead into the bathroom, the door open, the light on, her kiboodle on the sink and her makeup laid out on every flat surface.

"Let me go, Spanky." She kept on looking at her makeup, at the five tubes lined up like shotgun shells on the sink ten feet away.

She chose a pair of slacks from a pile on the bed and tucked her knees up to her chest, shot her legs into them.

"I ain't got to do a goddamn thing," he said. "You ain't going to be in no movies. Augustine gets drunk on a few wine coolers and next thing I know," he took a swig of the nearly empty bottle, "he's going on about how you going to have to leave some time. What's that about? You going to leave?"

"How much have you had to drink?" she asked.

"Never mind that, okay? I keep myself healthy. Maybe lately I deserve a break."

"Maybe you do."

"What's that mean?"

"I was agreeing with you."

"No. You said it different."

"Come on, Spanky. Augustine likes to talk. He says I'm going to be famous. I ain't going to be famous. That just doesn't happen. Spanky, you know him. I'm his gay crush. I'm his, his, Mariah Carey. No—" She grinned and palmed her hair. "His Whitney Houston."

"Then I guess that makes me your Kevin Costner cause your ass ain't leaving this room."

"Augustine doesn't fantasize about me cause it's true. He does it cause he wants it for me, and that's just cause he wants it for him."

Spanky angled his knuckles so the bottle's mouth pointed at his heart. "I got bones now, Kiddy. I got more bones than you or I could spend. What else do you need? I'll get it." He raised the bottle up and tilted his head back. It was

170

empty but for a few white bubbles tracking up its side. He looked at her and tossed the bottle into the laundry basket in the corner. The trashcan sat full in the opposite one. "You want to go?"

"I want to go tomorrow. I don't want to, like, go forever."

"Maybe they're the same thing. I let you out of my sight and you disappeared with that whiteboy for weeks. What about our deal?"

"You didn't buy me nothing for three weeks, I didn't give you nothing for three weeks. What about it?"

He weaved his head back as if she had him on the ropes. "That's not the deal I'm talking about." He opened his arms like he was calling a crowd for cheers and discovered there was no one around to root for him, "Was that all you thought this was?" He waved his hands away, head down that he'd almost gestured at what he really meant— himself.

She looked at the wall. At a picture of a fifty-nine Impala ripped out of Lowrider magazine and taped there like a piece of art. She whispered, "That's the only deal I knew about." She pushed her face into a pillow.

He brought his elbows into his ribs and showed her his fists. "You knew about that other thing."

"Do you mean the thing you only tell me anymore when you're drunk?"

"Fine," Spanky said. "You want to act dumb? You want to play like you don't know? I'll make you a new deal. You let me in that bed with you and I let you go. And I don't call you or page you or send for you or nothing. But then you do go. Then you don't see me. You sure as hell don't see whiteboy. And you don't set a pretty little foot back in Clearwater. You got that?"

She got up on her knees in the bed. "Why can't I come back?" She brushed her hair back of her ear.

"No."

"Why?"

Spanky ducked his head back, pulled his chin into his throat, was looking down. "Cause seeing you is hard on everyone I know. You're the thing. You're the thing. I thought it was him but it was you."

He began to undo his belt buckle, fumbling with it, his head falling forward, heavy and sudden, to examine the silver buckle and its engraved S. He got it undone and his baggy jeans fell away in the same moment, something thudding loudly on the floor when they did so.

She was craning her neck to see what had weighed down his pants.

"Don't worry. It ain't loaded." He took his shirt off and tossed it away. He put a knee on the bed and then the other. He took her small chin in his hand. "It's just for show. So," he whispered. "We got a deal?"

June had drunk his sight blurry and the streetlamps narrowing a train track across the sky bled out into the night as if light were a liquid. He squeezed one eye shut and with the other tried to lock onto Spanky's house, to see the window where the light had been shut off, and to figure in his head how long it had been since then. It had been a whole flask, he thought. Time is relative. Maybe ten years wasn't even that much so long as you didn't measure it in years.

Before he could condense the last few nebulous hours into any measurable quantity of time, something startled him, and he shut the radio off and cramped the wheel to see. What was it, a man? Someone coming down the sidewalk at a steady clip, a redtipped cigarette floating before his face. Too far to see who. But there was something wrong with that face—a man could see that from any distance—something seriously wrong. And the arm, the left arm, dragged much too long. The shadow threw the cigarette away. The red tip arced over the wet grass.

June watched closer, squinting that one eye closed again. He screwed the cap back on the flask and put it under the passenger seat as if sheer distance from the alcohol's source might make him sober. When he finally saw clearly the man's too-long arm was not the man's arm at all but a machete shimmering for an instant under a streetlamp and he saw simultaneously the man's face, his patchy mustache beneath the bare cartilage of a nose, a puckered eyesocket, not much left of the ears, and then back he went—man, machete, and all—into the stuff of shadows, which seemed poured out before him now like a hot asphalt track to Spanky's house.

All the house windows were dark. June got out of the car and waited to be sure the man didn't see him follow.

.

"No, Spanky," she breathed against his ear. He was atop her in the bed, her legs wrapped around his hips, but she still had her panties on. Her shirt was off though, and her bra. He took a nipple between his teeth. She said no.

He slid a hand in under her panties, over small folds of flesh and she exhaled.

She ran her hands up the back of his head and interlocked her fingers. She seemed to be thinking hard about something, brow furrowed, seemed to be trying by force of will not to feel. She began to cry, one neat track through heavy white powder back across her temple into her hairline.

"What?" He raised his head. He licked his lips. "What?"

"I don't want you to."

He brought his hand up and used his thumb to wipe away the new tear beginning to follow the same course toward her ear. Left a shadow of his thumb in her eye make-up. The air near their faces was heady, perfumed by her musk and his malt liquor breath, his sweat, her tears.

"I know what you were talking about," she said. "I know about that other thing. I wasn't playing dumb about us. But I don't want to. Not anymore. That's the truth."

"It seems like you do."

"But I don't. Will you stop?"

"Don't cry at me. Don't tell me to stop. I'll stop when I'm supposed to."

He backed away from her, the flared head of his penis smearing a glossy trail across the inside of her thigh. He tucked himself back in his shorts and stood up off the bed. He began to put his pants on but dropped them, the thud of the gun in the pocket, and went instead for his Everlast shorts balled up near the hamper.

He slammed his fists together and pointed at her. "You know what, fuck you. You don't cry and tell me to stop like

I'm going to rape you. Me?" He stumbled into one leg of the shorts, kicked through the other. "You can take your ass out of town now. Out of here, now, please."

He unlocked the locks on the door, clawing at them, clearly wishing he could burst through the door instead. He got the door open and stepped out.

The light from the fridge glowed across the kitchen floor for a moment, the beer bottles inside jingled when he slammed that door shut, and he left out into the backyard.

The dogs began to bark.

June thought, *And the hounds began to howl.*

The way June figured he had two options, and neither was all that good. He could wait it all out. Or he could jump on in. Maybe those were the only options anyone ever had.

He walked slowly toward Spanky's, not looking at the house which was his target, but looking instead up at the streetlamps, trying to better imagine the map of the yard, the few glimpses of the inside of the garage that he'd gotten while sitting on his ass in the dirt after Spanky's punch.

June stopped to listen—the dogs were barking furiously now—then sped up his pace. A howl drowned in a gurgle as if June were hearing it under water. One by one the dogs began to quiet down, and the night, which had seemed on some verge of explosion, became still.

Only the sound of June's footsteps on the asphalt. Then someone padding toward him.

He'd gotten within ten feet of the front yard when he could be sure the creature rasping and limping out of the dark was not a crawling man.

The dog loped down the slope of the driveway. Coughed blood across the whitewalled tire of Spanky's Buick. It came toward June, a dark bubble forming beneath its throat, a darker bead traversing its surface.

The dog whimpered, staggered a few feet closer, and collapsed.

June went on up the driveway.

A dead dog lie sprawled at the front of the Buick like the night was a hot one.

It wasn't. June's breath clouded the air before his face.

Many of the dogs lie in dark masses, some of them huddled against each other, dead or breathing their dying breaths—none of them even whimpering now.

The whimpering was coming from the garage. The large front door was closed and locked, but it was bordered by light, and somewhere in back, a block of light fell out over the kennels.

177

June came through the yard, past the empty grand-stand, looming over the macabre scene on the ground. All of the kennel doors were open. Not all of them were empty though none of the shapes within stirred.

From a telephone wire running overhead crows cawed down at the pit, but June did not look up.

He went on around back of the garage. On the top of the fence, a rim of concrete had been set with broken bottles standing in it—a poor man's barbed wire fence. Blood made stained-glass of the shards.

June thought Spanky was alone by now. He hoped so, too.

The garage door was made of a light wood and he only had to tap it to make it swing inward. But when he looked inside, a red flurry burst out and he swatted at the mad bird and it lashed at him with forked feet and finally flapped up and over him onto the fencetop. He watched the rooster strut there on the fence, avoiding the glass shards with ease. All aflame in the moonlight, somehow red and cool blue, it warbled but did not crow. He touched his cheek where a thin line of fire ran, looked at his fingertips and saw no blood. The rooster strutted on the fence, taunting him.

The next time he tried to open the door, he pulled his hand back like he'd been burned and, it fell shut. It creaked closed as he leaned onto his thighs, spitting into the dirt.

He stood and breathed deep. In the garage, the whimpering became harried and frantic. He pushed the door open again. He tried not to look into the pleading eyes of the butchered dog at Spanky's feet. The prized dog, looking from June up to—though June could not follow its gaze—its master.

The garage was as it had been except for a shiny chrome cage two by two feet with chickenfeed scattered on the cement at its open door. The sawhorses supporting the cheap shelf of jars filled with jerryrigged medical tools and supplies. The limbless mannequin wearing Spanky's butcher's apron, the pale blank face an impression of June's.

A collection of bottles stood neatly around the leg of Spanky's chair.

A boxing magazine lay open, some of the pages crumpled—it had been dropped from his hanging hand.

A steady drip from the limp fingers onto the magazine, a picture of a young man holding up a belt he'd won.

There was little blood on the ground. A bottle half full of beer had rolled cleanly on its side to the belly of the pitbull, which lay on its side in turn, and showed June a gash from throat to chest. The dog's eyelids were thick as velvet. Its chest heaved.

June stepped over the whimpering dog and went to the mannequin, tried to remember, Five across, five down? He wasn't sure.

He took a vial though and went to the shelf and took a syringe.

He sat in his haunches before the dog, pulling the plunger back, removed the needle from the vial, put it in the dog's thigh, and depressed the plunger. The dog tried to turn its head back to watch June's hands but yelped, and instead rested its head on the cement.

After a while the dog shut its eyes and stopped crying.

When he heard Kiddy scream June nearly fell back, onto the cold cement floor.

He scrambled up onto his feet with syringe and vial both still in his hand and though he was sprinting out the door he shut the light off as if the dark in the garage might seep into him, to hide the image of Spanky sitting there, head back, bare-chested except for the blood hung like a cloak from that deep, dark collar.

He found Kiddy speechless and pale. Her hands were down, palms out, seemingly showering in the moonlight, looking anywhere but at him or the dogs.

"Did you do this?" she asked. She fanned her eyes.

"Hell no I didn't do it, but that don't mean we can hang out here for people to think we did." He took her by the elbow.

"Where's Spanky?"

"Let's go." He wrapped his arms around her waist and lifted her up, and began to walk her away as if she were a statue he was claiming.

"Where's Spanky?" She slapped his face and head.

"Spanky isn't here."

They both looked up when the rooster flapped its wings and hovered a few staccato moments in the moonlight. It perched again on the fence. It strutted, head bobbing.

June let Kiddy loose. "He's not here, okay?"

She straightened her clothing. She twisted around her wrist a watch that wasn't there. "Okay."

The Ghia was parked next to Brenton's Ferry in the lot out back of the complex. Its windows were steamy. Where drops of condesation fell, lines of color tracked after, thin lines of sight to the couple inside.

Kiddy was sitting in June's lap, crying. She had her arms up around his neck and her face buried deep in his chest. He was cradling her, saying *shhh, shhh,* and humming an old song.

She said, "He wasn't that bad."

He stopped humming.

She sucked tears off his neck and cried more to replace them.

June rocked her in his arms. The old leather seat creaked and cracked beneath their weight.

"He wasn't that bad." She stopped crying and was silent for a long time. He smelled her hair. He kissed her forehead.

She said, "He wasn't."

He realized, June hadn't ever said he was.

TWENTY-FOUR

Brenton said:

I got a call about some strange shit down near Bixler, just a couple blocks from home. Normally the SEACCA dudes deal with dead felines and rodents and shit. Even the bigger ones. The dogs. The horses in Norwalk. The farm animals that belong to all the wetbacks in the barrio. But I guess they were taxed. This day, they called out the fuckin cavalry.

So, anyway, I said bye to Mary and she like smiled in this way that said she was coming over that night, which she's been doing more and more, and I been drinking less and less. I left kind of sad, kind of wanted to stay. Kissing on my woman, hell, doing anything, beats chaperoning dead people. But a part of me had to head out and see the circus. Word was around that day, this was strange shit.

I was rolling fast through the hood with the uniform on and my Locs down against the sun. I was laying, just laying on that horn. People done recognized the roach coach for what it was now, the Ferry, and no one liked to get in the way of the dead. People turned out my way like they did for the cops, quicker maybe, traffic just parted like they were scared I'd bring them with.

When I got to the house I knew right away all the trouble was at Spanky's. Saw his sweetass Buick Regal parked up in the driveway. The cops ushered me into the crime scene like I drove an airplane. Both sides of the street was blocked off and people weren't allowed out their homes. There were sheets all over the street, like a bunch of ghosts just laid down and died a second time. Every one of them sheets was stained brown with blood. A rooster was crowing.

I saw my buddy Mike, the cop. He was smiling.

"Park over there, bro. You gotta see this."

I stepped on the brake. "What's under those sheets?"

"Whoa-ho-ho, brother. You are way warm. You're like Tapatío hot." When I'd parked and got out he was leading me around counting each sheet in Spanish, counting whatever was beneath them with a real bad accent. "Un-oh. Dose. Trays. Kwat-row."

Rusty clouds filled the sheets like rain coming.

I asked, "Are these what I think they are?"

There were sheets in the driveway, one in front of the Regal, a bunch on the lawn and in the kennels. The pit in the yard was empty. For a second I thought someone had dug it like a mass grave, like they show all the times on the History Channel, to throw all these things into, but run off before they got a chance. But there was blood all splattered and staining the wooden walls and I thought no, maybe these bodies had been all dug up. But then I thought, who would do that? And besides, wasn't no pile of dug earth and no shovels around. And would have taken twenty shovels or a caterpillar.

Then I saw the cops all crowded around back of the garage. I heard the rooster crow again. I looked up and it was hopping around on the wall, the broken glass at its feet sparkling just like diamonds. A big red rooster screaming at the sun.

"What's with the bird?" I asked.

"Hell if I know. It's the only thing got us out here, though. Neighbors said they put up with parties and all kinds of weird noises but they'd be damned if a rooster was gonna wake them up at the asscrack of dawn."

The rooster puffed its chest out and shot its head forward and crowed louder than a siren.

Mike said, "I don't blame them. I'm about to shoot the bastard myself."

"Where's Spanky at?" I asked.

"In there," Mike said. He pointed at the garage and the cops gathered at the back door. "His head's barely hanging on by a flap."

I smacked my lips. "Why you gotta talk like that, fool? That's a human being."

"Sorry, man. Sorry. You gotta laugh or this shit'll get to you."

"Yeah, well, maybe it already has. You don't see me laughing."

The cops started to back away then, some of them cursing and moving faster with each step.

Out from that crowd of four or five cops comes this sheet, moving on its own, bloody as hell and swaying forward, into the yard. After a second, I saw the paws beneath it, and I knew, just knew, this was some dog come back to life. Maybe it was Spanky resurrected to come vengeance himself on Clearwater, and about to start with me for listening to a cop make fun of his chopped-up head or talk about killing his rooster. Then the sheet got caught on a wheelbarrow's handle by the garage, and the sheet pulled away from this poor cut-up pitbull, maggots already mov-

186

ing on his skin like if you could see his muscle moving when he walked.

I said, "Goddang."

Mike said, "Stop that thing."

But no one stopped it and it went across the yard to the kitchen door. There was a water dish there and it started drinking.

Mike said, "Guess that's one less for you to take. SE-ACCA'll get it. That's the one we found next to Spanky. Only one Spanky didn't keep in a kennel. You know anything about these dogfights here?"

"Nope."

"We don't got any next of kin. We got a number for someone named Augustine, you know him?"

"Just some guy you see around."

I turned and walked back through the yard, the driveway, toed the sheets up to see beneath each one. Each one a pitbull, scarred up bad and dead.

Mike followed me out, his belt leather creaking and cuffs rattling the whole way.

"What you want me to cart them in?" I asked him.

He's all, "The ferry."

"That's messed. No special bags or boxes? I chaperone human beings in the Ferry."

"Chaperone? You crack my shit up, Brenton. No difference between dead dudes and dead dogs. Couple more calls, few more years, you'll see."

I just stood there, kinda shaking my head.

"Denial makes you crazy," he said. "Loco. Insane in the brain."

I went to the back of the Ferry, opened the doors, and took down the gurney.

"Hey," he called to me. He was looking at me over his lowered aviators, real serious, all business now. "Just toss them on in. No time for that shit, understand? Toss them in."

TWENTY-FIVE

The scarred man who'd killed Spanky and the dogs had gone free because everyone blamed it on June. The cops, once again, could pin nothing on him, so after a month or so people began to say that June was untouchable.

But June had described the killer to the cops. He'd owned up to being there that night. He showed up at the substation each day to find out if anything new had turned up. Was it that hard to find a man with no nose and no ears and an asshole for an eye? When he left after one long afternoon of questions he heard the secretary whisper to an off-duty cop in a flowered shirt, *There goes the man you've all been looking for, I don't care what it is, but he's done it and more than once. I went to the simple meal at church last Wednesday, and Rachel told me her sister said . . .*

June began to hear the voices again, anytime no one was speaking directly to him. If someone did address him, he often didn't hear, listening too hard to everyone else all the time. At night he lay on the red couch cradling the guitar like a woman and wondered what he had intended to do to Spanky the night of the murder. He hadn't intended to shake the man's hand and call it good, that was for sure. But he hadn't intended to kill him. Had he? He began to imagine the killer as a version of himself, an other, and believed somehow that if the man was caught it would redeem him. Separate him once and for all from the man this town thought he was.

He drove the Ghia five minutes up Clearwater. Into Huntington Park. It should have been called little TJ because Everyone who walked the streets was brown. The streets themselves were named Florez and Avenida Luz and Calle Trece, some he got and some he didn't. In mariscos restaraunts and banda clubs, La Gigante supermarket, he spoke with the cashiers. He spoke broken Spanish and they spoke broken English, the men always frowning and the women always batting their eyelashes, but he couldn't find the man with the scars.

By the time the cops had a good lead on the killer, he'd crossed into Mexico, and that was that. June's other was gone, off the premises, lost in that near south that was somehow worlds away. With no one to take the blame for Spanky—and the dogs, people seemed most upset about the dogs—the people of Clearwater went back to blaming June. From petty theft to armed robbery, from faceless rapes to murder, there was no mystery left. No mystery at all. June done it.

Once, Walter told June that he saw a man who lived across the street drive home drunk, and squish his daughter's white cat. He'd scooped the thing up with a shovel, crossed the street, and dumped it under the Ghia's tire. The father hadn't even bothered to wash the guts off his sedan's wheelwell.

June replaced La Llorona, El Cuycuy, and the Bogeyman when parents told their children scary stories at night. Better listen to your daddy and be home by ten, or Junie Walker's gonna get you, June heard them whisper.

People got wind that June had worked in the forest and a story went around about a big fire the summer past, a story mostly true about a whole unit of firemen being burned alive, and the less true but more popular ending that June had simply strutted through the flames unscathed. Come to Clearwater to burn it down too. People said he couldn't be killed.

Nothing could have been further from the truth. June knew it. Maybe Kiddy did. Maybe Brenton and Walter had an idea. The truth was that June began to feel more vulnerable to attack than he ever had, and the more he thought about Spanky's death, something in the story comforted him.

He just had to make the right decisions, keep the story playing out, and it all would come together in the end. Something would come for him as it had come for Spanky—not necessarily to kill him—but it would come out of his past and come out of the dark, finally, to shear off his other.

Well, then he was waiting for it. He stopped hearing the whispers. He slept fourteen hours a day in peace and comfort on that big red overstuffed couch. He spent most of his time awake playing guitar, writing songs for an album that was thirty songs deep and not a note of it recorded on anything but an old tapeplayer with a sticky play button.

TWENTY-SIX

He still met Kiddy out in Hollywood but she came back to Clearwater less and less. She often begged him to stay with her out there, but his urge to drive home and wait for his fate—like one would wait on a package from a loved-one; though he had no love-ones this made him all the more desperate to receive it—grew too strong in the middle of the night. He would end up driving drunk most nights, swerving on the empty 710, making an impossible game of avoiding potholes to keep himself awake.

He went with her once to a party at the Whisky A Go Go. There were two levels to the club and the party had the run of the top level and its bar and the backstage dressing room. June and Kiddy leaned on railings and shouted into each other's ears what few things they had to say to each other.

"What are you drinking?" She held up her cosmopolitan by the glass's delicate stem with a pinky out. She'd taken to wearing less makeup. Her eyebrows were growing in and she hadn't drawn them on like stab wounds in weeks.

He lifted his short glass.

"Big surprise." She kissed him on the cheek. He lifted the glass to his lips.

One of her new friends knew the band on stage, a leatherclad aquanetted scarfstorm revival of eighties rock. When the set was done they all went backstage to party.

The door they passed through dropped them into the dressing room. The only lights were single red bulbs hanging from chains here and there. There was a long dark hallway to a heavy-looking door with EXIT painted on it in paint that had dried dripping. June was filled with the sense, had almost breathed it in like cold air, that there were big houses beyond. Neighborhood streets. Families sleeping.

In the dressingroom, a man in a fringed leather jacket took a baggy of cocaine from a pocket and knelt on the gray carpet before a glass coffeetable.

"Hollywood." June sat on one of the many ragged and stained couches. "What's with all the glass coffee tables?"

No one seemed to hear him.

The music in the room was there by radiation, it hummed in the walls and ceiling and floor. It seemed to hum in the bodies, of which there were plenty and too intertwined to count. Kiddy wasn't the only one dancing, but she was the only one anyone paid attention to.

She was dancing on the glass coffee table, white powder at her feet. She was wearing lowcut jeans and a tank top. When her hips swayed you could see either hip bone, and the quartered muscles of her abdomen drew her belly button in and June could not bring that small hole into focus. The man with the spiked hair was kneeling before her with a straw, snorting cocaine from around her toes. June remembered the cold weight of the whiskey in his hand and drank it down. Set it beside his foot and a slender bare foot was there too.

He eyeballed foot to calf to leg and by then knew he'd never reach any clothes. There was a wispy blonde triangle of hair where the thighs folded into belly. He looked for face and, only after many more moments of hapless searching, pink nipples on small high breasts, a thin arm draped now over his thigh, found a young woman smiling at him.

Around the room, other girls were naked now. They had become increasingly so the more coke and liquor they discovered. But not Kiddy, where she danced at the center of it all.

Her eyes were closed and her hands in her hair, dropping into a sudden crouch, and then slowly unfolding herself up into a towering widelegged stance, hair flung back. She no longer kept her hair stiff with hairspray. Thick ropes of it undulated at her shoulders like live things.

A voice said, "Do you want to touch my breasts?"

June looked back at the girl to his side.

"How old are you?" he asked.

She put a long finger on his lips and said, "Sssh." Her eyelids were dark with eyeshadow, and in the red light they shimmered whenever she blinked. She blinked slow.

"Touch me," she said. "I'm in a revolution. A sexual revolution. I slept with five men this week. Me and my boyfriend had a threesome."

"Congratulations."

"Thanks. Touch my titties."

He reached across himself and cupped her right breast. She shuddered and she was a bad actress. He was looking around the room, "How's that?"

"Yeah," she said. "Oh yeah."

It was like thumbing a small pebble. He lowered his hand.

"Yeah." She grabbed his crotch and he felt himself thicken but he wasn't happy about it. "Yeah?" she asked. "Yeah!" She said. "Right?"

He looked at her, her eyes shut behind patches of eyeshadow like bruises, so he shrugged, and said, "Yeah."

Both men and women had begun to crowd Kiddy, her gravity drawing them to her center, drawing her own arms around her body while she danced. The men and women danced in pairs, but occasionally one of them would reach a stray hand out and run it up Kiddy's leg. The music outside was reaching a climax, the walls shook and the lightbulbs swung in parabolas on their chains. Faces appeared and faded so that to June the whole room seemed walled by countless faces, countless expressions, and he squeezed his eyes shut.

When he opened his eyes everyone was smiling. Maybe they had been smiling to begin with and he just hadn't noticed. June studied the faces of the men and women surrounding Kiddy. He found their eyes restless.

June stood and tugged Kiddy by the elbow. When she'd come down off the coffee table and kissed his neck, a strange feeling began to creep through him, a feeling like guilt but hotter, and unconcerned with other's ideas of him or any notion of sin. He'd altered something here, something he wasn't supposed to.

The band outside had quit playing their last song. The people in the room began to shift nervously as if somewhere someone were blowing a whistle beyond the pitch of the ears, but not the body. The girls crossed thin arms over their breasts. Men began patting the car keys in their pockets. The room smelled and felt like a sour mouth. One by one, people left, on down the long dark hallway, to the black exit door that once it was opened would suck them outside into the cold world of no longer night and not yet morning.

Then a gliding ride in the back of a rich man's limousine, to drink in a club with red waterbeds on a rooftop, and the Last Waltz projected on the wall of a skyscraper across the street while carlights traveled at the bottom like an electric river in some steel canyon. He'd stare, wishing to see everything up close while one of Kiddy's co-stars tried to put the moves on her or him or both of them at once, one rednailed hand on the railing, another in his pocket. He'd wish you could climb or hike down this canyon, but at the bottom of the stairs all it was was another street, blurry lights in his eyes, numbness in his gums and lips, and the acid taste of cocaine way up high in his throat.

One morning he stood in front of his apartment door, trying key after key, until he fumbled and dropped them. When he stood back up holding them in his hand, Daisy stood there with her hands behind her back, smiling into one cheek like she'd done something wrong.

"Kiddy's not here," he said.

"I know." She swung her hands around front and showed that she was holding a stack of papers. "She doesn't really ever call me, anymore." She changed her footing. "Hey, I remember that you liked to write songs. And I, I've got this screenplay I've been working on. Would you like to maybe read it sometime? We could meet for coffee in a few days and talk it over."

He canted his head like a cameraman and furrowed his brow, and smiled. He'd never looked at her this long before, he realized. She did too, and she tugged the hem of her shirt down though it hadn't moved an inch. He thought of bed, first alone, then with another body beside him. Her body. He rubbed his forehead hard.

Daisy. Now that would get them all talking. Maybe even saying nice things, she was so sweet, though he couldn't be sure. His reputation could just end up singing her own like a flame creeping at the edge of a nice, clean, white sheet of paper—it would become hers. So that even if she wrote the most beautiful script there was, no matter how alive, people would smell its carbon, see the char, and it would remind them of its imminent death, and of so of their own.

"Long night?" she asked.

He nodded.

"Well," she said, "I'll leave you alone. Think about it."

When she was halfway down the breezeway, he said, "Thing is, I wouldn't be any help."

"Oh," she said.

"Yeah," he said. "Sorry," he said, but he wasn't. He was smiling. And he went inside and slept better than he had in weeks. When he woke the next morning that peaceful feeling was gone, the events of the last few months crowded around him and spoke his name into hard black telephone mouths. He was a stranger at a payphone. Or he was the payphone. Or he was the homeless man being beaten with the payphone over asking for a little change.

He made a decision. Even L.A. felt too far. He knew he wouldn't return to Arizona, either. Not until that settled and peaceful feeling had come back to him. So he spent most of his time in his apartment writing songs.

That's how Augustine found him.

TWENTY-SEVEN

He was hunched over his guitar on the carpet in the empty living room, so intent on scribbling in his notebook that he didn't look up when Augustine barged in and set a caged rooster down on the carpet.

June raised the pen—"Shhh. Let me finish this verse"—but he never set the pen back to the page. His face relaxed and his eyebrows rose and he was smiling. "Nevermind. It's good how it is."

"That's my cheddar." Augustine was holding something in his right hand and gripping his silver rose beltbuckle with his left. "Stand up."

"One second." June was dogearring the corner of the page.

"Junie. Stand the fuck up, man."

When June looked up he saw Augustine pointing an odd, tumescent pistol at him.

"What the fuck is that?" he asked. In all of Clearwater, in all of Los Angeles County, only Augustine would own a pistol shaped like a cock.

"What the fuck do it look like? Man, it is a gun."

June set the pen in the notebook and folded it closed, all the while shaking his head. He leaned the guitar in the corner of the room and when the head hit the wall the guitar resonated sloppy dischord. He stood slowly. He was aware of the rooster clucking around in its cage, but he was eyeballing the strange pistol. "What's that on the end of it?"

"Don't worry about it, man."

June crossed his eyes down the barrel.

Augustine said, "It's a silencer. Don't you know a silencer when you see one?"

"A silencer?"

"Yeah, man, now be quiet so I don't have to silence you." Augustine passed his eyes over the bar that separated living room from kitchenette. He read the label on each bottle and either nodded or tsked his response to each. He finally studied the living room and seemed not to notice June any longer, was squinting, and he was gnawing his soul patch with his top teeth. The thin jawline beard seemed a strap to some mask of frustration, his face lacked the usual cool playfulness. "Where's my couch?"

"In the bedroom."

"In the bedroom!" His voice rose into the jagged falsetto that seemed better served to singing. "What you got it in the bedroom for?"

"To sleep on."

"I picked that couch out, special, for this room. Especially."

"Sorry."

"Yeah, you are."

"What do you want, Augustine? You want the couch, you can have it." June began walking toward the bedroom, but Augustine raised his other hand to grip the pistol and adopted a widelegged crouch with one eye closed and the other squinting up against the cocked hammer.

"You done me wrong for no reason, Junie. You done Spanky nasty. I warned you, and I didn't think you'd be the one to last, you know? But you did, and something about that gives me the tummy rumbles. I can't sleep no more, Junie. I see you. I see what you did to those dogs. I see what you did to Spanky. It ain't right. You got to get yours."

June couldn't quit staring at the oblong barrel of the pistol. Then a look of recognition traveled down his face from brow to mouth, a slackening as he sighed.

"Man," June said. "Is that a potato?"

Augustine aimed the gun at June's face. "I told you, it's a silencer."

"It's a russet potato."

"It ain't russet." Augustine held the gun back to look at it. "It's Idaho gold, motherfucker."

June nodded. "Oh, well, I see the confusion. That's just the brand. See, Idaho Gold is still technically a Russett—"

"Shut your mouth, Junie, I ain't playing no more!" Something in Augustine's voice sounded ready to break, as if the man and not just the voice had hit a pitch it could not sustain.

June thought that Augustine could kill somebody tonight. Maybe not most nights, but this one—no doubt. June put his hands up. "Let's sit down. Let's talk about this. Just you, me," June nodded at the cage, "and that rooster." He recognized it now from the night he'd found Spanky dead. Here it was again, and June didn't like the omen.

"Where we gonna sit, Junie? You done took the couch into the bedroom."

"Let's just have a drink. Relax. I got some good stuff. You want some Patrón?"

Augustine shook his head.

"Some Black Label? You like Black Label?"

"They should call it all brown label. Whiskey tastes like shit." Augustine flicked his tongue in and out of his lips like there was a bad taste in the air. "How about some of that Bombay Sapphire? You got that Bombay Sapphire?"

"I got Tanqueray."

"Alright. That then."

Augustine sat crosslegged in the corner of the room with the gun pointed at June behind the bar.

On the bar, behind the bottles, June had a different kind of collection. He had the gnarled safety-pin Kiddy had used to stab him. He had an old tape of his music that he hadn't listened to in years. And he had the vial and the syringe he'd used to put that prized dog of Spanky's out of its misery. He tried to look casual as he began mixing their cocktails.

The dark crescents under Augustine's eyes looked like bruises.

"You look tired," June said.

"I am tired. Look at my eyes, man. I got crows feet, bags, and saggy lids. I done tried Vitamin E. That shit don't work. I look at least two years older than I am."

"That's too bad."

"Why'd you do what you did? I told you to stay away, Junie. All you had to do was stay away. Why didn't you?"

June brought their drinks over and made as if to hand one over but Augustine raised the pistol. June crouched, set the glass down on the carpet, and backed away. He lifted his own glass to his lips and drank. The ice cubes clinked when he lowered it. His mustache was wet with the drink and he cupped his lower lip over it. "It's wintertime," he said. "You should be drinking dark liquors."

"That like a fashion thing? Like labor day and white?"

"Not sure. Heard it somewhere."

Augustine gripped an ankle and dragged his foot back so he could lean on a knee. He groaned when he reached out and took up the drink. He raised it along with an eyebrow and took two big swallows.

June sat crosslegged where he'd been before, staring at the guitar in the corner and the notebook before it as if he missed them. He wasn't too far from Augustine. "I didn't do all that shit you think I did. I didn't stay away neither, but I didn't kill Spanky. The cops even said so."

"I don't give a fuck what the popo say. I got a aching belly. You know what it's like at all to have a belly won't quit telling you something?"

"Lately my gut's been telling me I'd have been better off alone in a watchtower playing guitar, than ever coming back to Clearwater."

"Belly's are right. Mine says you came back, got my pad, got Spanky's girl, and got the rest of your life. Meanwhile, Spanky's dead, and my cheddar ain't enough to feed a goddamn mouse. You want to know what I got left, thanks to you?" Augustine sloshed his drink toward the cage. Inside, the rooster spun around and strutted to the opposite end. "You looking at it. A meanass uglyass rooster. Don't even lay no eggs."

"Rooster's don't—"

"It was a figure of speech, bitch. I know a goddam rooster don't lay no goddam eggs. Point is, I got so little dinero I couldn't buy a eggmcmuffin from the egglayingest chicken on earth."

"That what this is about?" June asked. "You gonna be the kinda guy who kills a man for money?"

"There another kind?"

June didn't say anything. Just sipped his drink whenever Augustine sipped his own.

June said, "I don't know you. You don't know me. But I'm telling you the truth. You ought to just go. If you want money I'll give you what little I have left. I made some big mistakes here."

Augustine started laughing. It was a playful laugh, a bit drunk too, and when he leaned his head back against the wall he slammed it. It looked like it hurt. He rubbed the back of his head and twitched a look over his shoulder once or twice, said *fucker* to the wall. "I told you, Junie, I know your type. You fuck shit up and you keep fucking it up cause you stubborn. This ain't about you, its about all the you's."

"All the me's?"

"Yeah all the you's. You all. You got to own something you done, man. You got to own something. But you wanna just move back to Timbuktu with a fuck you Augustine better luck next Spring? Ha. Your kind is all the same. You ain't gonna let Kiddy go." His head nodded forward and he jerked it back up. "Ain't gonna let me sleep." His eyelids were a shiny gray, the circles near black beneath them. "No, mister music man. Oooweee. Right behind. You ain't going nowhere."

Augustine set his glass on the carpet, elaborately casual, a pinky raised. In his sudden drunkenness, he advertised his intent to shoot a whole second before the shot came, and June had already dived onto his back behind the bar. He was looking up when the gun fired and the blast was swallowed, like an explosion deep underground, and clumps of potato splattered the walls, the ceiling, and there was a gap in the blinds where the bullet left through the screen, potato pelting June's jeans and boots. The rooster was flapping against its cage like newspaper caught in the wind. When June sat up Augustine was still in the corner, staring at the pistol in his hand, stunned and covered in mashed potato.

June started patting himself clean. Augustine made an attempt to do likewise that tottered him onto his side, and he smashed his face into the carpet. He spilled his drink with a clink when he reached for it with the pistol still in hand, then dropped the pistol and righted the glass. He smiled when he saw he'd done at least that much right.

June stood over Augustine for a while, shaking his head.

When June reached into a back pocket and took out a handkerchief, he didn't say anything.

When he reached in again and removed the small vial the contents of which he'd mixed into Augustine's drink, he said, "I'm sorry, Augustine, but you were gonna kill me. I didn't want to, but... I'm real sorry," and he tossed the vial onto the bar counter.

He sat on his heels and wiped Augustine's face with the handkerchief. He wiped around the eyes, closed now, so heavy and steel gray a crowbar couldn't have opened them up. June kept on shaking his head.

"It's a silencer," Augustine whispered. He was smiling. "Supposed to make everything go shhh..."

That's when Walter knocked on the door. Said, "Junie, what's going on in there?"

Walter said:

I was bound and determined to get that pool cleaned out. Just my body didn't share my zeal. So I thought it was time to catch hold of Junie once and for all, and see if he might help me like I helped him by letting him stay here, by taking his pay on a year's rent and no one wanting him to stay. So I was headed over his place anyway when I heard what sounded like a popped balloon. And after I knocked and called out, it took a while for him to open up. When he did, I said, "What's going on in there? You setting off fireworks?"

He smiled and looked inside and I tried to push my head in to see but he was in that doorway like an earthquake might could come at any second and he said, "I was baking a potato in the microwave. Dang thing blew up on me."

"Oh that ain't a problem," I told him. "It'll clean right up. Now I got something I need to talk to you about."

He thought for a while and then he let me in, and I'll be damned if it didn't look like the apartment had been wallpapered with potato salad.

"Damn," I said.

He just shook his head and said, "It's a real mess."

"You the king of understatement. It's FUBAR."

"Sorry I can't offer you anywhere to sit," he said.

"That's alright. Courting that lady seems to keep you busier than any job could. I guess a man in love don't need the creature comforts."

"You think that's true?"

"I love my wife more than anything but I'd say it's because of her I need all the creature comforts I can get." I kind of just looked around and chose a spot to sit down on the carpet and I could tell my back wasn't gonna let me get back up. I put a hand down to brace myself. "Carpet's wet right here."

"I spilled a drink. When the potato exploded."

"Huh," I said. "So I saw Augustine come in here."

"You did?"

"Yeah, before I went inside to tell Kayla I'm gonna go at that pool this week. Once and for all. It's a real eyesore."

"It's not too bad."

"Like Aunt Holly's famous Walltaters ain't that bad neither?"

June took a seat Indian-style across from me.

"Well. I know Augustine got interesting ways of making his money…" I must have rambled for a good ten minutes before I got around to saying it. "You think you could lend me some marijuana?"

Junie just burst out laughing. He almost choked on his own spit he was laughing so hard. "Shit, Walter," he said. "Is that what this is about?"

I told him keep it quiet. Said I didn't want no one, not even Kayla, to know. But I been down to the library, done some research, found out maybe a puff here and there could get me working more.

There was noise then sounded like from the bedroom, a thud, and we looked at the bedroom door for a long time. We kept scanning back from the door to each other, back to the door.

"It's a nice place, Walter," he told me. "But the walls are thin as hell. I hear the neighbors go at it noon and night."

After a while he got up and went to the bedroom and I could hear him shuffling stuff around.

June closed the door behind him. He was trying not to look—not at the rooster, a large red stone, asleep in its cage in the corner, and not at Augustine, whose torso had slid off the couch, and who was currently perched against the carpet on his forehead—but June in the end had to look anyway, just to get what he needed. He got on his hands and knees beside the couch and reached beneath it, smelled the dusty carpet. He slapped his hand around in there for a while. His own breath bounced off Augustine's face and came back, somehow more stale; that's how close he was, and he shuddered.

Finally June felt the cold metal case and pulled it out. From his knees, he unlatched the case and raised the lid.

Augustine's coke, some weed left in plastic baggies, a glass pipe, a small mirror, a pack of straight razors. A few plastic lighters. June palmed the pipe and a baggy and a lighter and shut the case.

He stared at the sticker. 'My Girl Likes to Party all the Time,' it said.

June looked at the back of Augustine's tweaked neck, the stubble of his fade, said, "Is that a good thing or a bad thing? You tell me."

Augustine's arms were hanging off the couch, pooling around his head, and June left him how he was. Then he went back into the living room to smoke Walter out.

Walter said:

We smoked off a little glass pipe run through with blue swirls. By my watch it took no more than thirty minutes.

But I'll be damned if it didn't feel like three hundred. I got to rambling about Kayla. About how my favorite thing she does is when she's listening to her stories and it's a real bad husband or man in one of them, she'll stop the tape and look at me until I notice she's looking. Then she'll smile at me and say, *Thank You.* I always ask what for but I know what for. So I believe I must have told him about that for a solid ten minutes and then I told him, "Well, you know all about that though. Right? You love Kiddy enough to make yourself the enemy of everyone in town. You might as well have had your way with Eve and eaten the apple to boot, the way people talk all that shit."

He looked all googly eyed at me and I said, "What? Old man can't say shit? Well shit. Shit, boy. Shit."

"I don't know," he said. "Yeah. I guess you're right, about the girl and the shit."

I chuckled at that, man. Chuckled more than I even should have, but I couldn't stop. Then he looked at me gumming my lips cause they were so dry and all I could think about was a glass or more like a bucket of water. I said, "I ain't smoked this stuff since I was . . ." But I didn't remember how old I'd been, and after a while I didn't remember I was trying to remember anything at all.

It was quiet for a long time. Then he told me this story. He said he was watching out for fires up in the White Mountains, and I started thinking this was that story that went around about him being in the fire and didn't get burned, but I realized quick it wasn't. At least it wasn't the way I'd heard it.

See, he was watching from this high tower and he said mostly all he'd do up there was play guitar and write songs and pine away for Kiddy. Sure, he'd had other girls, he said. But the more he thought about it, with his father's family a bunch of deadbeats, and his mother off in Mexico, he didn't have anyone really. And so Kiddy started to feel like the thing he did have. At least, a thing he could get back.

But he could tell the fire that night was different, that the winds were so bad it was like a wave of fire coming up the mountain, eating dense ponderosa, white pine, oak, and big tooth maple. Burning their boles down to red wires like kindling. He seen there's this herd of elk in its path, and also there's a unit of Hot Shots that'd been dropped in to cut line right near the elk. Well so he was at the very tip top of this mountain out of the path of the fire, but he could see it was gonna burn all the way up the side of the mountain until it got to this sheer drop and couldn't burn anymore. And that's where these elk started charging, straight toward that precipice where there ain't nowhere to go but down.

So he was trying to get the men on radio and he couldn't. Nothing but static or bursts of panicked men's voices. For some reason, he said, it's like he was meant to just watch these men survive or die. So some of the men start running after the elk. And others, they go their own way, banking northwest toward a rock face. See the men, none of them knew what they were headed to really, when they decided to follow the elk.

"It was like they all had to face this decision," Junie said. "Follow them animals, their instincts, or head up to that rock you been told could save you cause at least it won't burn, might cook you like a frying pan but might not. And they parted ways. And the ones who chose to do what their brains were told to do, they lived. And those other ones. Eventually the men were all a part of the elk herd at the edge of that mountain. And that fire was coming up toward them and a few elk tried to break through it like all it was was a wall or a fence and a moment later they'd come back out scrambling and covered in flame and their antlers like huge candleholders, the tips burning, and over the edge they'd go. I could see them twirl and tumble and even the wind couldn't blow them out. It wasn't hard to see what would happen to those men that thought instincts would save them. I didn't even watch, but I felt guilty about that."

June felt like they deserved someone to watch their last few moments, but not someone who was judging them. He said, after that, he just counted the days until the season ended.

"That true?" I asked him. I couldn't do much but ask questions. The idea of making a point seemed like harder work than I was cut out for just then. My forehead felt heavy and tight. "You were judging them?"

"I don't know what I think about them anymore. Tell you the truth I don't think it was them I ever thought about, other than to feel like shit on their behalf."

"So what'd you do after that?"

"Fire season ended. My daddy died. I came back here to bury him."

"And for Kiddy."

"Right. And for Kiddy."

"She's a good girl?" I tried not to say it like a question.

"Yeah, she's got a lot ahead of her, you know? She's still figuring out which way she wants it all to go." Junie had the pipe resting in his palm. "You want another hit of this?"

"No. No, no, no. I'm feeling real good. Think I'm gon-na get some work done. Then I think I'm gonna say hello to Kayla, if you get me."

"Get on with it then."

"Dirty till dead, that's what I say." It was nice and easy getting up off the floor, and the muscles in my back felt like they were soaking in hot water.

"See ya, Walter."

I had just touched the doorknob, almost opened the door and left out of there like I was alone, when something made me turn around and say, "What are you going to do?"

Then I realized I'd been wanting to ask him that from the get go. And not like, *what you going to do tonight?* But more like, *what are you going to do every night after?*

"Me?" Junie looked at the walls and pieces of carpet covered in white mush. "Clean this mess up."

One of us closed the door, I don't remember who.

TWENTY-EIGHT

June knocked on Brenton's door and you could hear Walter digging through the utility closet while June waited for an answer.

Eventually, Brenton stuck his bald head out and looked either side of the door. He had the telephone in his hand. "Junie? What are you doing here?"

"I need your help, man."

Brenton raised the phone to his ear and said, "Baby? Baby, I'm gonna have to ask you to wait a while. I got company." He looked into the house and cooed a few words into the phone before he shut it off and looked up again. "Get your ass in here, dog. It's been a minute."

The apartment was the same as June's, only it had furniture and lamps to fill out its corners. There was an old china hutch against the entryway wall that had belonged to Brenton's grandma. When the two boys would play over her house they spent too much time fogging the glass doors with their breath. The coffee cups, creamers, and coffee pot that Brenton's grandpa had kept in there, were all shaped and painted like breasts. Each one could fill a cupped palm, all but the jiggers complete with fluted brown nipples from which to drink.

Brenton went on into the living room and shut off the TV, the Lakers and Pistons shrinking to a star in the middle of the screen. The star blinked out.

Brenton sat on the large paisley-print couch, covered in plastic, and when he leaned back to get comfortable it crackled. June took a seat in the wooden chair at the end of the coffee table. He looked around at all the things Brenton kept out for decoration. Hundreds of unrelated trinkets on every flat surface or nailed to a wall. Postcards framed and hung like they were paintings. Key chains hanging from pushpins in a corkboard in the kitchen. Shot glasses galore on a bookshelf, no books. The books stacked instead beneath a coffee table draped with a folded-over serape in green, black, red and white and still more green. Raiders memorabilia littered the kitchen counter.

June patted his knees. "I like what you done with the place."

"It's filled out. Before you left I hardly had shit. I had that china hutch after my grandma passed, my grandpa's titty glasses, and this couch was theirs too. I had my TV and a stereo."

"It looks good in here."

"Mary been helping me figure out where to put things, too. Make it more . . ."

June smiled. "Cozy?"

"Yeah, well, cozy sound kinda gay but I guess that is the word. So, no beef or nothing, but you ain't had me up to your place. I remember you ain't never used to have nothing but a TV and stereo neither. And the guitar."

"I got a collection of liquor bottles. And the stuff you just said. I got a red couch I'm keeping for someone."

"That's cool, dog. You the rambling type anyway, right? Pick up at a moment's notice." Brenton snapped his fingers. "Like that."

They were quiet for a while. June began to say something but Brenton had already moved on, stood up, and gone to the kitchen. He took out two bottles of beer and stuffed one each in a pocket, then he took a pint bottle of whiskey from the freezer. It looked thick as syrup when he tilted it to the light. He disappeared into the entryway and when he returned he had two shot glasses shaped like breasts. He sat on the couch again and poured their shots. His fingers left prints in the frost on the bottle when he handed June a shot glass and raised up his own. "Hold on." He pulled the beers from his pockets and set them out on the coffeetable too. "Chasers. This whiskey was on sale at Albertson's. I don't promise it'll taste like nothing but cold."

June said, "When we were twelve we'd have given anything to fool with these glasses."

"Yeah, I never even use them. I think there's dust all over my titty."

"Mine too. Guess real makes fake pale in comparison."

Brenton looked puzzled. Set down the shot glass. "Now I know you can't be talking about clay titties no more. What's with all the deep shit?"

"Nothing. Let's drink. I bet the dust adds flavor."

They knocked the shots back and reached for their beers at the same time. Opened those and each drank about half.

"Brenton," June started.

"Hey dog, let me show you something."

June set down his clay titty glass and leaned. "Look, I don't have a lot of time."

"You got time to see this." Brenton stood and went down the hallway to the bedroom.

When Brenton turned on the light music blasted around the house and June saw that there were speakers hidden in the corners of the room. One behind a plastic plant. Another behind a framed, signed picture of Marcus Allen from ninety-three. The music turned off and the speakers were hissing.

"Just a sec," Brenton called from the room. "Here we go."

A snare popped in metronome for a half a minute while Brenton came back into the living room and sat down. Then guitar eased into the mix and the drums found a beat and a bass dropped in almost on time. It took June a moment to realize this was his song.

"You mix the rest into this?" he asked.

"Wait." Brenton had his bottom lip clamped between his teeth and was bobbing his head. "Wait."

When June heard himself singing, it sounded better than he was used to. It sounded fuller, nuanced, the way he heard himself in his head. On his own tapes his voice always sounded ragged and thin. But the real surprise came when the song reached the first break. All of the instruments dropped a step at a time into a groove, and two new voices sang the theme behind June. It was a man and a woman singing. Neither of them were on pitch but they were in harmony and they sounded like they belonged in the song. Only June could have noticed otherwise.

"Wait till you hear the next one," Brenton said. "I'd taken all this old music I still had, fed it through this cheap fourtrack I'd bought at the swapmeet, and me and Mary had done some backup vocals. The drums are weak. The drum machine I got is from the eighties so all the beats sound like Madonna and shit. My buddy, Mike, you remember Mike. He the cop. He played a little bass in high school so he laid that down. It's the bomb, right? I mean, I don't see why we can't lay this shit down in a studio, you know?"

"Look, Brenton. The tape sounds great but right now I need a real big favor."

"Oh. That makes sense, man. That makes a lot of sense."

"I'm in trouble."

"We're all in trouble, man. Don't you ever see that?"

"I'm in trouble and I got to take Kiddy to this premier—"

"Kiddy's the only one I know that ain't in trouble, homie. The only thing. She's fine. She'd have been fine without you coming back and she'll be fine after you've gone."

"I know. It's done between us. But I gotta do this last thing, and I can't cause I'm stuck with this big problem in my apartment."

"You ever told anyone a whole story, man? From start to finish?"

"What are you talking about? I'm telling you a story right now."

"Man, you ain't telling me a story. You're telling me a situation. You're telling me what you need me to know. You're telling me what's useful to you. I don't think you're selfish, man, I just think you're cold."

"You're probably right."

"I know I'm right. I've known you for how long, man? And I don't know shit about you. Alls I know I know from your songs. And you ain't even got time to listen to them. I could be with my girl right now, Junie. She does me good."

Brenton drank some more whiskey, this time from the bottle. When he set it down it was half empty.

"I been down," he said, "word is bone. As much as you been. Hell. Man. Maybe I been down more." He took the bottle up again and drank straight from it again, then leaned back with the bottle resting in his lap. "You know that old song from grammar school, says, He Lifts Me Up? You remember that? We used to change all the words to the church songs and make them dirty. Ha. Man, that's cause Jesus ain't never lifted us up. I been chaperoning dead folks up the freeway, down the boulevard, ain't seen no one lift them up neither." With his elbows propped on his knees, he hung the bottle there between his legs and sloshed the whisky around inside, watching. "You know who lifts me up? My woman does. She resurrects me. And here I am with you. Been gone ten years and back for how long and you ain't but said a few words to me. Who you lifting up, June? And if you don't know, who's gonna know when they got to lift up you?"

"Maybe here's your chance, Brenton. Maybe here's me asking you to do it?"

"You go ahead and ask me, dog. But it ain't my chance. Believe that. It's someone's chance to learn but it ain't mine. Have a drink or two with me before we do this."

"Don't you want to know what's going on first?"

Brenton leaned further forward, now face to face with June. "What's going on? Where do you think everyone else lives? You might spend most your time living in your head, but we all living in Clearwater when we get back from vacation. You think I ain't heard Augustine talking mess about you in the bar? You think I couldn't have warned you this would happen? Who couldn't? I saw him go up to your pad. I heard a noise. Then you come knocking on my door for a favor. What happened to Augustine, Junie? He ain't never come out of there."

"You always watch me from way over here?"

"When's the last time you gave me a different choice?"

"You're right. Since I set my mind on Kiddy, I been doing some fucked up things. You're right about me. I'm gonna tell her it's time for her to do her thing, you know."

Brenton spoke through locked teeth, "Leaving me alone with this is a fucked up thing. You want to stop doing fucked up things, then help me get the motherfucking dead dude out your pad."

June had a finger pressed to his lips but it was too late, Brenton had already said what he'd said. June stayed quiet for a long time, waiting for sirens or crying or anything that would mean tonight a man had died, would make it for real. But there wasn't nothing like that. If anything, Brenton was what changed.

With his fingers clamped tight on the bridge of his nose, Brenton looked like he was fighting just to stay awake and June knew what had tired him out. This friendship.

June said, "You don't have to help."

227

"I don't have to do shit. But if you want some body to get a shortcut to the mortuary you better have a few drinks with me, I don't care how little time you got."

"Are you sure you want to drink before?" June asked.

"That's the only thing I'm sure of."

June stared at the now-empty bottle of whiskey in Brenton's hand. He said, "Augustine came at me. I asked him not to. I didn't want to."

Brenton watched him in silence. June finally said, "Alright then. Pour the shots."

"No. On second thought you go on and do it yourself. Leave the keys to your car case I need it. Take the ferry. Bring it back right away. I don't want to be seen with you no more. I don't want anyone thinking bad about me. Better pretend you never came by."

"I don't get it, Brenton. I just told you the story. You said I'm cold but I'm telling you the story."

"That ain't the whole story, dog. Un-uh. There's more left. And I don't want a part of it."

Walter stood there holding the hose so the water arced out into the pool, splattered at the bottom. He listened to the splatter for a long time. He had a smile on his face when the water began to shift the windrowed hair around the

228

pool's bottom. He just stood there, holding that hose in one hand, the other in his pocket, and that big old smile on his face. Once or twice he flicked the hose side to side so that the water snaked a path through the air to land on any piles of hair that hadn't yet been soaked. He didn't do that too much though. The motion made him dizzy.

In the breezeway above, his door opened. Kayla called down to him but he didn't look up.

"What on earth are you doing?" she called. Somewhere a set of blinds zipped up.

"Look like I'm doing? I'm filling the pool."

"But it's full of that muck."

"I'll be able to just skim it off the top once it's full up."

"You'll never fill it up with that hose. It'll take all night."

"I got all night to do it."

"You're crazy, Walter. Word's gonna get around and they're gonna put you in a home."

"If word gets around it's cause you're chasing it. You tell them who cleaned this pool. Tell them. Tell them mystery's solved." He snickered. "Walter Lee done it. With the hose. In the courtyard." He began to sway the hose side to side in a soft and rhythmic arc, his paunch jutting forward, the smile on his face growing. "And another thing," he called.

"Cook me up something good. Like some scrapple. Or a fried egg sandwich."

"Cook? It's evening," she called. Her voice cracked in shock or frustration. "That's breakfast food."

"I don't care if it's midnight, cuddlebear." The hair at his forehead was wispy in the small breeze that sometimes got trapped in the courtyard, and that same breeze misted his face. He tamped a thumb onto the hose to fan the water. "Look at me," he called. He tilted his head back as far as it would go and they looked at each other upside down. He said, "I believe I've worked up an appetite."

When the door slammed shut, Walter watched as if to be sure she was gone. She was. He stared at the railing before their blurred door for a while. Then at their door behind the blurred railing. "Thanks, baby," he told her.

Brenton's door flew open and June stepped out into the courtyard. It shut hard behind him. June nodded once to Walter and went up to his apartment, and his boots were loud as he went.

TWENTY-NINE

When June got to the mortuary he didn't know to park in the back alley, so he parked out front on the neighborhood street. He smiled to himself when he remembered the small victory at his father's funeral here just a few months ago. Then he frowned. He couldn't remember why it'd mattered so much to have his father to himself. Barely even remembered, Mamma had been there, too. It felt like a barfight or a woman taken home drunk who he'd hardly recognize the next day. Life felt like this, every day of it—drunk, as he was, on anger.

June had won, though. He remembered that clearly.

The houses around here looked nice enough, but who'd want to live near so many dead people? The yards were mostly overgrown with trees or boxed in by hedges and he figured this was one of the things neighbors did to block their eyes day to day.

The clock on the dash said it was five til five. He wasn't going to make it to the premier in time. Hell. Kiddy would get over it.

He took the keys from the ignition and separated out the key to the mortuary, a large bronze duplicate with Do Not Duplicate imprinted on one side.

He slunk between the two seats into the back of the Ferry and knelt down to undo the knots in Augustine's sheets. When he was done with the knots he unwrapped Augustine, slightly in awe, mainly melancholy, at this mummy he'd created and was unraveling.

June hefted Augustine up, cradling neck and knees like you would a child, onto the gurney. Augustine's arms flapped off the edges. June stuffed each of Augustine's hands into a tight white jean pocket. When would he get cold? When would death freeze him? June didn't want to be around to know and he threw a blue sheet over the body, hopped outside and shut the rear doors hard.

He knocked at the burnished oak doors to the mortuary, pressed an ear to a spot or too.

Knock, knock again, nobody home.

So he slid the key into the lock and heard the tumblers' turn reverberate through the building.

Then he opened the door just enough to slip inside.

Brenton had told him there'd be a workshop somewhere near the back of the building, and June tried to find his way in the dark, took at least three steps before he clocked his head on an unlit lamp jutting from the wall. He thought maybe he'd been ambushed by some gauntlet-clad security guard, cursed, and shot a hand up to touch the lamp's cold medieval shape. The lamp was crooked and he thought *Damn, I got a hard head. Barely touched the thing.* He smiled and laughed at himself. *Lot of people would agree with you about that first thing; tonight you found yourself one less.*

A sound crept from the end of the hall. Or maybe a feeling, a hum.

He was sure that somebody else who could count themselves among the ranks of the living was in this building with him. But you couldn't feel that, could you? Must have heard it. Heard a live man living.

Creeping down the hall on the balls of his feet, a finger trailing along the wall to keep his distance from vicious attack lamps, the clink of metal on metal grew louder. He was right beside it, or on top of it, the source of the sound. Clinking, scraping, occasionally somebody humming a tune June recognized from his youth. One of Brenton's favorites. He reached a door at the end of the hall and set his hand on the doorknob.

The sound of a motor now, whining. Was that giant corpse wrangler taking a saw to some poor body? A rickety saw at that, June was thinking, when he opened the door slowly, one eye closed and one open.

In the alley, Brenton was leaning his back against the Ghia's driver side door. The motor was whining that it wanted turned off, put down, taken out of its misery.

"This car's a piece of shit," Brenton said.

"What are you doing here?"

"This is my job. In a way, I got a agreement with some folks."

"I got it taken care of."

"No you don't. You bring the people back here, not through the front. The front's only for living people."

"Does it really matter?"

"To me it does."

Then a door to June's left swung open. It surprised June to see a door so close to this one, they seemed like they could only be two doors into the same room. But a hulking figure stepped out of the doorway and into the alley and June could hear his breathing, as if all that flesh grew not only outward, but inward to obstruct the very functions that kept it alive.

Sam said softly, "What are you doing here?" When Sam turned to look at Brenton his wattle shook. "Why is he here?"

Brenton said, "He was just leaving."

June said, "No I wasn't. I can do it myself."

"You can't," Brenton said. He reached inside the Ghia and withdrew his folded uniform. He stepped into the legs one at a time. "You were right to ask me. So go. Let me handle this, fool." He tugged the legs over his tennis shoes and zipped the front up to his throat. "There's things I can do that you can't, you know?" He smiled and held the car door open not like a chauffeur, but like an usher. "Go on to your premier."

"What is this?" Sam asked. He stepped forward, swallowed the distance between him and June whole, and gripped June's arm. Before June could pull back he felt his forearm already going numb.

Brenton said, "Sam, let him go."

"No. He nearly lost me my job. Playing that game he did in my mortuary. Misposting times. Taking a priest hostage. Who do you think my boss blamed that on?"

June tugged his arm but it wouldn't move. He felt the man's fingers like the solid face of a vice.

Sam said, "I'm calling the cops."

Brenton and June shouted at once, *No.*

Sam tugged June's arm hard, and let go. Though June expected to strike the wall and hazily collect what little there was left of himself to collect, the wall never came. He landed instead on his tailbone, a pain that felt white, slightly ticklish, and made his teeth taste like powder. And for a moment he felt fortunate to be at the top of the cold steps sinking into the dark behind him, until that moment left him all but alone with the steps, and the realization that he still had their full length to fall.

He ended up about six feet down in a dank smelling room with gurnies in rows and bodies on some of them, and a large green elevator door in one wall. He saw all of this before the pain set in, and then he couldn't open his eyes.

The door shut. He heard it lock from outside.

He found his feet but when he stood he wished he'd learned to live without them, cursed and gripped the backs of his legs. They'd taken most of the steps in the fall. He climbed the steps on hands and knees in the dark, stood, and pounded on the door. At first he thought the feeling seeping through his jeans and t-shirt was his blood, soaking into the cloth, but it was just the cold that belonged to this place. It crawled around the floor like a fog. It would be colder near the bodies on the gurneys, he was sure, and he pounded on the door and yelled, "There's dead men in here. There's dead men in here, let me out."

After a few long minutes, he gave up. He felt his way back down the steps to the elevator door. He was shivering, teeth chattering. On his hands and knees he swept one hand along the elevator door's edge until he found a leather strap knotted at the end. He tugged it up, stood, and let go the strap while the door continued its disappearing act into the ceiling.

When he was inside the dimly lit box he pressed Lobby and listened to the gears turn, watched the doors close, waited to ascend.

Brenton had nearly convinced Sam to leave things alone when June burst out of the open door into the alley and landed on Sam's shoulders, punches clapping against the giant's fleshy neck and head.

"Are you crazy?" June yelled. "There's dead men in there."

Sam crumpled to his knees with June still punching, though the punches landing less often, sliding slick with hairgrease off the mortician's head and ears and cheekbones. Brenton kicked June and June rolled away, stood, breathing heavy and ragged. Sam collected himself into something like a standing position, and with so much to collect it took a long a time.

Brenton kicked the Ghia's door, "Get the hell out of here, Junie. Just go on."

"I don't like it down there, man." June was pointing at the door to the workshop, though they all knew what he meant.

Brenton said, "I'm telling you to bone out, man."

Sam said, "No one but me goes down there." He jabbed a thick thumb at the door. "No one but me and them."

"What the hell's that supposed to mean?" June yelled. He showed the mortician his fist and the big man slumped back. "You trying to scare me?"

"No." Sam adjusted his collar and tugged his tie straight. "I'm not superstitious. Are you?"

June jabbed a thumb into his own chest, "Hell no."

Sam looked at Brenton but Brenton wouldn't look back. He was staring at the ferry, at its closed doors and what was behind them. "What?" Brenton looked up. His eyelids wouldn't quit flapping. He looked lost, as if he'd been somewhere else for a moment and only the question had brought him back to this alley, this situation.

"Superstitious?" Sam asked.

"Me?" Brenton said. "No."

Walter, who'd succeeded in filling the pool, but not in skimming it clean, had come into the house demanding dinner, nearly choked, he ate it all up so fast, and fell asleep in his recliner right beside Kayla's with one hand cupping her breast.

Kayla had stolen the keys easy enough.

June folded himself into his seat. The movie was half over but he'd been shifty since he'd left the mortuary. The dark of the theater made him think of driving in the night, never being quite sure of how many miles you were eating up, and not a single good look at the places you passed.

"After the movie," Kiddy whispered, "We're all going out. You're coming right?"

"No," he whispered. The air around her smelled like perfume and rubbing alchohol. "I don't think so."

"Shhh," she said. "My scene's coming up."

It was hard for Kayla to separate out the key to Junie's apartment. Her fingers were swollen from knitting all day and she looked anxious about being outside. She got the

239

door open, peeked into the dark. Then she hit the lights on the empty apartment.

Some strange white substance plastered the walls and ceiling. *What on earth,* she mouthed.

She looked back down either side of the breezeway before she went inside.

Kayla sniffed around the living room a while, made a sour face. "Like skunk," she said.

She moved forward and snooped around the bar counter, rolled her eyes up into her head like to calculate how much Junie must drink daily based on the collection of bottles. When she locked eyes on the bent safety-pin on the counter she sucked both lips into her mouth. When she spotted the small labeled vial, cracked but not broken, she grinned. She picked it up and turned it round and read the label.

Sublimaze.

"Druggy," she grumbled, set it down, and went straight for the bedroom door.

It was closed, and she was careful not to make any noise, tiptoeing to it as best as she could. She'd always been proud of her lean figure, and she arched her back like a cat with only a few cracks to be heard. At the door it was easy to hear, there was definitely something making a raucous in there.

A struggle, maybe. Grunts.

Kayla placed her hand on the knob, pulled it away like the knob had burned her.

Behind that door, she must have thought, is more answers than I can stand.

She went to the bar and took up a half full bottle for a bludgeon.

She had the bottle gripped by the neck when she touched the knob this time, and she twisted the knob and pushed the door open all in one big shot.

The grunting was louder still and she screamed, raised the bottle, looked all around the room.

Screamed again as if it would ward off any attack by sheer volume. But her scream woke the rooster and the cage shuddered when it flapped and kicked and pecked to get out—furious now—crying not its morning call, but something entirely different. Something straight-up mean.

When Kayla saw the rooster she stopped screaming so fast her teeth clicked. The cap fell off the upside-down bottle's top and whisky glugged out onto the carpet, soaked her slippers. The grunting had ceased when she'd screamed and the rooster had panicked, but now that the rooster had shut up the grunting started back up again. Right along with mattress springs' whining.

Kayla went to the wall and put her ear to it, had her left eye shut tight and her cheek fighting to meet it. Wrinkles fissured the straining portions of her face. She listened to the couple next door for a little while, and then all at once she deflated. She was quite small in that mostly empty room. A cage not three times as big as that rooster's would have held her.

She dropped the bottle at her feet and said, lamely, "Oh hell."

Her slippers squelched whiskey as she left, and she closed all the doors behind her.

Brenton said:

I got Sam calmed down and back in the mortuary before things fell apart. I wasn't in the right headspace. I couldn't even look at the dead dude. He didn't seem right. Was warm, but it takes a while for them to cool down. It was something else. He looked peaceful and that ain't the way they normally look. I don't care what they tell you at church, peaceful is Sam's job. Think Sam would be loaded as he is if everyone that died looked happy? Hell no. Sam makes them look peaceful—death just makes them look dead. And I couldn't believe how small he was. Built just like a little girl.

Like I said, I was drunk, and drinking more. And I couldn't stop thinking about how it would have been better if I'd never taken this job. I don't know what I'd have done but it wouldn't have been anywhere near this. And that's what I was muttering to myself: "What are you doing? What are you doing?" And I was taking the gurney down out the back of the coach when this girl walked up to me. A little girl out playing by herself in the alley. With a dolly and everything. Guess her parents was at the Mariscos restauraunt. It sounded real busy over there and that dumpster was smelling bad that night too. I told that little girl I was working. I told her.

"Get out of here," I finally shouted, when she wouldn't go. I get real mean when I drink whiskey. But still she wouldn't listen, wouldn't go away. I yelled, "Get out of here. I'm working. It's important work I'm doing here, okay? It ain't kid stuff."

But she was real snotty, right, like braces that showed when she stuck her tongue out at me. And she kept trying to look inside the truck and I said fuck it. And I just pulled the gurney out and said, "You want to see then? You want to see what I do?"

And I guess I pulled too hard.

And the wheel on the gurney stuck, tilted the gurney over.

And Augustine's body tumbled down the ramp, and I fell all tangled up with him and that collapsing gurney. And shit. I ain't heard anyone scream as loud as that girl did right then.

Kiddy elbowed June and pointed at the screen just as he recognized her in the blond wig and behind all the make-up. She was screaming bloody murder when an axe's shadow rose up behind her, the camera zoomed into the shadow, and the shadow fell to end her scream.

"How'd I do?" She had turned to face him. Was smiling so wide it seemed that part of the theater was suddenly a little brighter.

"Great. You did great."

Outside, he stood at the open rear window of a black limousine. The car's paint job reflected the theater's marquis, but shattered, and all the people walking by looked fluid.

Kiddy sat inside with a few men and women, most of which June could only see as a weavework of bare legs and black pants. She leaned out the window and kissed him on the cheek.

"Sure you don't want to go?" she asked.

"I'm sure."

"You okay, Junie?"

He smiled and she seemed eager to trust it, to recede back into the limousine as he'd said and meant he wanted her to.

The limousine pulled away, her small hand waving daintily out the window before it too receded, then the whole car was swallowed into traffic on the boulevard.

Brenton said:

The little girl dropped her doll on the asphalt and ran into the restaurant, not out and around but straight through the metal service door and for a second all I could hear were knives on cutting boards, banda music blaring from a dollar store radio, the clanging of pots and pans. I wanted to push at that dead dude and his gurney weighing down my legs.

Wanted to, but now he felt too heavy. And I couldn't get my legs out from beneath him neither, and when I tried to talk to him it wasn't like normal, where I feel like they're listening. It was just this silent, heavy weight, pushing down down down and wasn't no way I was gonna get up.

But then a big shadow fell over me and Augustine. I looked up and Sam was standing there, and it's like for once I saw him for as big as he could be.

He tossed the gurney to the side.

He picked Augustine up off of me with one arm and used the free one to help me up.

When he'd got Augustine on the gurney Sam didn't even ask me no questions. Just wheeled him on in, business as usual. And I got in the passenger seat of the ferry, and asked Mary to come drive me home after she got off work, cause I wouldn't drive that thing no more. Not for no body living or dead.

THIRTY

June stood in his suit, tie undone, shirt buttoned only as high as his chest, waiting for Brenton to answer the door. He hadn't worn anything but the suit for going on two nights now, since the premier. He remembered reading somewhere about the Beatles' album cover of Abbey Road—that they were dressed as a funeral procession. This should have creeped him out of wearing the suit, but it didn't because in the album cover the one in the black suit is the priest, the one in the white suit the deceased, and June's suit was black as his mood.

When the door opened it was Mary, and she was smiling, and you could hear Brenton laughing at something playing on the TV.

"Hi," she said. "Just a sec." She turned around and waddled back into the living room. You could hear her kissing Brenton real loud.

After a while Brenton came to the door. In the china hutch behind him the set of breasts was complete. June smiled and Brenton looked over his shoulder. When he looked back he said, "Whatsup, Junie?" and shrugged.

"I'm sorry."

"Don't do that, man." Brenton smacked his lips. "Whatsup?"

June reached into the chest pocket of the coat and pulled out a brown manila envelope folded around something square. "It's my newer stuff. I like what I heard of the other. But it don't matter. I trust you to do something cool with it."

Brenton took the tapes. "Thanks, dog."

"How'd it go earlier?"

Brenton looked over his shoulder again. "I don't want to talk about it."

"Sure?"

Brenton nodded. "Word is bone. But you ain't got nothing to worry about."

"You think you'd want to come with me to the movies, like old times?"

"No thanks. I got my girl over. We're watching a movie right now anyways. Maybe next time."

"You been with her a long time?"

"Going to be." Brenton smiled. "Turns out she got together with Walter's woman, they got to talking, and I'm hooked up managing this place with the old man."

"Good. Let me hear the tapes when you finish with them."

"Peace." Brenton had almost shut the door when he pulled it open and said, "Hey Junie."

"Yeah?"

"You gonna go to the movies anyway?"

"Yeah."

"You always liked everything old, man. Movies, music. That's something funny about you."

"I guess it is."

"And you don't mind doing things out on your own. That's something I wish I could do." Brenton looked inside and when he looked back at June he was grinning.

"Yeah, right," June said. "But I ain't heading to the movies alone. I got a chicken's gonna go with me."

"You just broke up with Kiddy and you already found a new chickenhead?"

"No. A chicken. A rooster. I'll take it with me. I gotta let it go somewhere, I figure over near the drive-in's a good neighborhood. Lot of Mexicans live there. They'll find something to do with it."

June knew he'd be late to the movie but he spent ten extra minutes walking around the pool, watching swatches of hair float around on the water like moss, a blue light glowing beneath the dark matted surface.

He went to the diving board and stepped up onto it. He stepped out to its edge and sat down, let his dress shoes just graze the water's surface. A wet lock of hair stuck to the toe. He lay back on the board and it creaked, rocked, was still, and he listened to Brenton and Mary's faint laughter.

He closed his eyes.

In a forest somewhere there were two eyes glowing like embers in the dark. They weren't attached to any creature, they floated free from place to place to see what was worth seeing. They saw a fire climbing a mountainside, chasing men before it, licking at their heels. Some men turned round, ran headlong into the fire hoping to pass through, were consumed by it. A man tried to escape it. Clothed in fire, he ran off the edge of a precipice, into an endless deep, the fire burning his hair like one hundred thousand wicks, breathing and crackling as the fire stripped him naked of cloth and skin, the wind of his fall whipping the flames to new heat he never knew could be. Still, more men fell behind him.

But that was no consolation. Or shouldn't have been. There was, after all, forever and ever to fall.

June sat up suddenly, shaking his head loose of those thoughts.

When he stood, he was fighting a smile, and that drew deep lines on each side of his red mustache. He was in the mood to play, friends or not.

He set the board to bobbing, sank, rose, sank, rose, and he was dying to test it some more. He imagined Walter, pointing a shaky finger and saying, *Careful, now, careful,* but a smile on his old face. He imagined Brenton just cracking up, shaking his bald head left and right.

And the first time he caught some air, he was grinning big. The second time or third time, he did bust out laughing. But by the fourth time, weightless as he was, it felt like he'd dropped his guts somewhere down below and all his blood was pouring after.

In that brief moment of contact, the diving board had groaned, Walter and Brenton disappeared, and though June wanted to change direction, though he wanted now to stay in the air and never have to touch down, though this time he wished his fall would take ten times ten more years, it only took that moment.

And when he landed, a faint crack moved through June as if it were the sound of something breaking within, of bones splintering.

He staggered, waved his arms in circles while the board bobbed him up and down. A patch of hair had floated away like a lily pad and the blue pool light on his face looked half as icy as he felt inside, sweat beading down either temple like condensation down a glass. After a while the diving board steadied and the weightlessness was replaced by something else, something close to sinking, maybe even shame, and he shook his head again, said *Damnit, June.*

All it is, is water. Water and some pretty girl's hair.

He laughed at himself, lamely, and then he crossed the diving board, the courtyard, and went upstairs. Headed up to get that rooster the hell out of his bedroom.

THIRTY-ONE

They were strange figures on the path beside the traintracks, he holding the tether and the rooster strutting before him. Its head swinging forward with each clawfooted step, pendulum like, as if testing pieces of the night that June had yet to reach. They looked stranger still as he walked the wall around the drive-in, cradling the rooster against his side like an abused familiar, what feathers it had ruffled. Its chest inflated near to bursting. That one blind eye shelled white.

June watched the screen every now and then and had to balance himself with an arm out to do so. When he got to the old man's yard he stopped. He stood there looking down through the trees, the nearby orange, the lemon, the vast avocado. He could see their fruits hanging here and there like ornaments for some strange holiday or lonely commemoration.

He stood on the wall for a long time, trying to see if the man were in there somewhere waiting for the moment to avenge his love, or festering in thoughts, wild thoughts, thoughts only an insane brain might stew.

June closed his eyes.

"One," he began to count.

"Two."

He didn't count loud, but he spoke the numbers to himself.

Behind him the movie was coming to its close. The music was at an insurmountable crescendo and the camera was panning away from a man and woman, to some sunset in a world where the sun set in black and white.

June counted all the way up to eleven, past that, before he stopped counting and turned to face the screen. There would be another movie starting soon. There always was.

The old man sat on his porch in the dark. He watched June sitting the top of the wall, his wall. An interloper.

The old man held the shotgun tight in both hands, one at the stock, the other on the muzzle, and pressed it cross-wise onto his thighs, as if only its power and weight could keep him from rising. He looked back and forth, from June on the wall to the door he could enter if he chose to go to bed. He stared at June for a long time.

Out there on that big screen beyond June's dark shape the credits were rolling. The names of the cast falling down upon June, as if he were caught in some strange storm of words, of people, the words pummeling him and still he would not go.

The old man stepped out into the glow the silverscreen cast upon his yard, and was step by step painted in greyscale. He raised up his shotgun. He aimed the gun high, perhaps even at the screen, and looked back at the door to his home again, as if one warning shot were all that kept him from peace and sleep and dreaming.

"Okay," he whispered. He gummed his lips in silence for a while. To someone, not himself, he whispered, "You'll be okay."

June watched three cholos walk across the lot toward him, wallet chains swinging at their hips. They wore baggy shorts and big Pendleton jackets. They walked with a wide step and their chins up as if they preferred to examine everything before them from an angle they'd predetermined as superior. The one in the lead was holding a forty ounce bottle wrapped in a brown paper bag. He elbowed his companions and they headed toward June.

A few feet from June, the rooster sat the wall at the end of its tether. It was quiet. June stared into its shining black eye. When it turned its head and showed the white one June looked away.

"Hey fool," the cholo in the lead called. "Where you from?"

June laughed. "I'm from right here."

"I mean what set you claim?"

"I'm from right here, man. I don't want any shit. Someone out there does. Go find him."

"Let's go," the one in the lead said. Before they'd gone too far he turned, tilted the bottle over his mouth and swallowed. He lowered the bottle and belched. Then he took a long step toward June and chucked the bottle into the air. All three booked it, ran toward a long silver Lincoln waiting in line at the exit.

The bottle arced toward June, shining, turning, and crashed against the wall a few feet away. That's when the shotgun blast came.

In one version of the story, June tumbled into the parking lot with a sudden heavy sound that had no echo and no resonance. A mist flared like a bright light across a camera lens.

The rooster had been dragged behind, like an anchor to the wall, flapping and struggling before it too fell. It flapped on the asphalt for a while, spinning on the end of its tether. It found its feet, tried to leave the ground and did so for a moment, before June's hand raised a bit and both hand and rooster flapped hard to the pavement. The weight was too much. The rooster tried again and had June's arm off the ground before both arm and bird slapped down.

The rooster strutted to June's outstretched hand, where the tether was wrapped round his index finger in a loose loop. The rooster began to peck his hand. Stopped for a moment. It cocked its head sideways, its bloody beak glistening.

It stabbed its beak at June's hand until the bone of a finger showed through. Beak gutted palm. Its beak was red and the few feathers round its head and chest matted and wet. It hovered long enough to strike June's head with spurless feet before it landed on his bloody back, and pecked at the holes from the buckshot.

It strutted over his back for a while, flitted its head to one side, then the other. Its good eye was a shining black globe. Nothing but red all around it.

In a sudden fit of panic it flapped and took off running. The loop came loose of June's finger, the tether slapped away over the asphalt, and then the rooster was gone.

But in the more popular, if not truer version, it was the rooster that was blown off the wall. As much as they'd wanted their stories to kill June while he was alive, once he was dead, they wouldn't let him sleep.

They said:

The old man grinned down there in his yard, holding his smoking shotgun to his neck like his departed lover. Convinced he'd caught the bastard, he'd shoot no more. The scarred and wounded bird had turned into an atomic accumulation of feathers, so focused and intense as to implode and suck after its departure the surrounding bits of debris, the wayward versions of stories, words, intentions that made them up, and lastly June, who went away again, leaving Clearwater perhaps not as he found it, but as it needed to be, rapt, distracted, busy telling stories, ignoring the lives the town would have otherwise lived all along.

THIRTY-TWO

Brenton said:

Guess I had one more ride to go.

I got to admit, it's nice, homie. Cruising with you like we used to. No chaperoning anymore, man. This is cruising. That's the one condition of this ride.

Shit makes me want to roll out to Uptown Whittier, look at the girls dressed for the club. Ha. Don't tell Mary, dog. Maybe after, go to Tam's Burgers for those bomb chili cheese fries.

I know I said I was done with this job, but when I heard it was you, I said friends do favors. Stop. Look. If I wanted that lip I'd pull it. No apologies needed. Not between homies. Well, not usually. But, I guess the truth is I do gots to apologize to you. I know you had beef with your pops, but that shit was between y'all, so I got to say this.

See, the day I took your pops in to see Sam, I had forgot my uniform. No disrespect, man. I just forgot. But then I asked your pops not to tell you. And now you're gonna see him. I guess word travels. Anyway, I'll make it up to you.

For one, this here, I won't tell no one about it. I'll tell them all you just left. Maybe back to AZ. The Smoky Mountains, right? Or was it the White Mountains? I'll tell them you liked the peace of all that wilderness and shit. I'll tell them you asked me personally to say goodbye for you. *Spensa mensa.* I got it covered.

It'll be better this way. Sure everyone'll spread the *chisme* about you for a little while. Spread the cheese like Velveeta on a cracker. But I'll stick to my story and that'll be the one that lasts. This, this here, ain't no one gonna know about it but you and me and the holy ghosts between us.

So guess what that is on the radio? That's you, man. I brought your tape along for the ride. A short one, true.

Here we are already.

I leave you in the good hands of my man Sam. He won't hold nothing against you. He believes once we die that's it. I don't believe that shit, homie. We all got to go somewhere.

Charon's Ferry Transportation Services' last stop. This your last ride and mine too, for a while. But I'll see you when we see you, man. Word is bone.

THIRTY-THREE

Sam stood hunched over June's body where it lay face down on the gurney. He was digging at the buckshot wounds that cratered June's back with thin hookended needles. He had his morning cup of coffee, a mug the size of a small vase, balanced on a stool at the head of the gurney. He was breathing loudly through his nose.

Augustine was on a gurney behind Sam, and parallel to June. Sam hadn't had a chance to look at Augustine once. The body looked in good shape and it wouldn't go anywhere.

Augustine's manicured hand twitched once. Then it lay flaccid again beside his thigh.

Sam, intent on June's body before him, squinted at the small lead pellet rising against the skin just beneath the shoulder blade. He couldn't seem to dig it out from beneath that ridge of bone.

Behind Sam, Augustine's hand twitched again.

Sam picked his huge mug up off the stool and sipped. Sucked air into his steaming mouth. When he moved to set the mug back down Augustine moaned behind him and the mug never quite made it back to the stool, just shattered on the smooth cement floor of the workshop. Sam watched the puddle grow toward his shiny shoes, seemed unwilling to turn around.

Behind him and blurry, Augustine sat up straight, twisted his head from side to side as if to unlock frozen joints. "Where the fuck am I?" Augustine whispered.

Sam turned then. Studied the small dark man, from his precisely trimmed facial hair, down the length of the sheet to the highheeled snakeskin boots.

Sam said, "You're in my workshop."

Augustine peered around Sam's massive shoulder, at June's body on the other gurney. "Did I do that?"

"I doubt it, sir."

"What do you mean?"

"You've been here all night. He just got here this morning. I guess you weren't dead."

"No shit I ain't dead. What are you, dumb? Where the fuck is here? I know, I know, your workshop. But where's that?"

"The mortuary, sir."

Augustine yelped and clapped a hand over his open mouth. He ripped the sheet away from his body and let it fall from him, staring at it all the while as if it were diseased.

He looked down at the gurney upon which he sat, yelped again, hopped off that and ran to the corner of the room as if the gurney too were the cause of this new and intimate relationship with death.

A scalpel glinted on a polished tray nearby. But when Augustine shot a hand out to take it Sam raised a fist and Augustine accidentally knocked the tray, the scalpels, clattering to the floor.

Sam said, "Please don't do that, sir."

Light rimmed the edges of the door at the top of the steps. Augustine craned his neck to study it. "Where's that go?"

"Outside."

"Outside?"

"Yes, sir."

"Will you let me go?" Augustine had his hands clenched together as if he were praying.

"By all means, sir."

"That's my cheddar," he said as he bolted to the stairs. He took eight steps in two bandy-legged bounds and burst out the door, sunlight washing into the room around him, consuming him.

The doorway burned bright and empty.

Sam squinted at the light with an upraised hand.

He stepped around the puddle of coffee and took the steps of the staircase laboriously, one by one, and reached one hand out into the light to pull the door shut. He took the steps of the staircase one by one back down.

He stood beside June's body.

Sam's shoulders fell away from his neck when he sighed, and he said, "I'm sorry about that, sir. Where were we?"

Christopher David Rosales is from Paramount, CA. His first novel, *Silence the Bird, Silence the Keeper,* won him the McNamara Creative Arts Grant. His second novel, *Gods on the Lam,* was published by Perpetual Motion Machine Publishing. Rosales currently lives in Denver, and is an Assistant Professor at the Jack Kerouac School at Naropa University. Contact him at www.christopherrosales.com.

For more information on Broken River Books,

please visit:

brokenriverbooks.com

Twitter:

@brbjdo